VICTORY
VS
REDOUTABLE

Ships of the line at Trafalgar 1805

GREGORY FREMONT-BARNES

First published in Great Britain in 2008 by Osprey Publishing,
Midland House, West Way, Botley, Oxford OX2 0PH, UK
44-02 23rd St, Suite 219, Long Island City, NY 11101, USA
Email: info@ospreypublishing.com

Osprey Publishing is part of the Osprey Group.

A CIP catalogue record for this book is available from the British Library

ISBN: 978 1 84603 134 2

Page layout by Ken Vail Graphic Design
Index by Alan Thatcher
Typeset in ITC Conduit and Adobe Garamond
Battlescene paintings and gunnery sequences by Giuseppe Rava
Digital artwork by Ian Palmer
Gunport views by Peter Bull
Originated by PDQ Digital Media Solutions
Printed in China through Bookbuilders

11 12 13 14 15   11 10 9 8 7 6 5 4 3 2

The Woodland Trust
Osprey Publishing is supporting the Woodland Trust, the UK's leading
woodland conservation charity, by funding the dedication of trees.

www.ospreypublishing.com

Editor's note

For ease of comparison between types, imperial
measurements are used almost exclusively throughout
this book. The following data will help in converting
the imperial measurements to metric:

1 acre = 0.4 hectares
1 mile = 1.6km
1lb = 0.45kg
1 yard = 0.9m
1ft = 0.3m
1in. = 2.54cm/25.4mm
1 gal = 4.5 liters
1 ton (US) = 0.9 tonnes

Please note that in order to avoid certain confusion, no
attempt has been made to supply the equivalent French
and Spanish terms for the weaponry and ships' features
referred to herein.

A note on the sources

Quotations of first-hand accounts appearing in substantial
form were drawn from the following sources, expanded on
in the bibliography: Fraser, Lavery (*Nelson's Navy*), Lewis,
Robinson, and Warwick.

Artist's note

Readers may care to note that the original paintings from
which the battlescene colour plates in this book were
prepared are available for private sale. All reproduction
copyright whatsoever is retained by the Publishers.
All enquiries should be addressed to:

Guiseppe Rava
Via Borgotto 17
48018 Faenza (RA)
ITALY

Web: www.g-rava.it
Email: info@g-rava.it

The Publishers regret that they can enter into no
correspondence upon this matter.

CONTENTS

INTRODUCTION

The Napoleonic Wars (1803–15) represent the high-water mark of the age of fighting sail, typified by that most majestic engine of war, the ship of the line, on whose fighting ability depended the balance of power at sea for the whole of that troubled

period. This study seeks to examine the function and role of the ship of the line, specifically at Trafalgar, where on 21 October 1805 off the south-west coast of Spain, 60 such vessels representing Britain, France and Spain fought the greatest naval engagement in history.

In May 1803 the Napoleonic Wars opened with the renewal of the Anglo-French struggle that had begun in 1793 and which had ended with a brief period of peace in 1802–03. British strategy depended, as always, chiefly on the Royal Navy's ability to confine the enemy's fleets to port by means of blockade or, failing that, to pursue and engage in battle those fleets that managed to put to sea. Between 1803 and 1805 the French did not, for the most part, venture out of port, so although British trade routes stood largely unchallenged, the nation remained under constant threat of invasion, for the French fleets at Brest, Rochefort and Toulon stood intact, albeit dormant, protected by harbour defences. These fleets thus posed a permanent potential threat in the form of what contemporaries called a 'fleet in being'.

Spain remained neutral until October 1803, when Napoleon forced her into an alliance whose terms required her to supply more than two dozen ships of the line for service in conjunction with the French, and by the end of 1804 she was at war with Britain, thus increasing the pressure on Britain's considerable, though severely stretched, naval resources. Were these scattered French and Spanish squadrons to combine into a single, substantial fleet, their sheer numerical superiority over any single British fleet could secure for them the few days' command of the Channel necessary to enable Napoleon to convey his massive invasion force, mostly camped around Boulogne, the short distance to England in a specially constructed flotilla. Herein lay the significance of the Trafalgar campaign.

CHRONOLOGY

1803

18 May   Britain declares war on France, formally opening the Napoleonic Wars.

23 May   French announce first tentative plans for invasion camps along the Channel coast.

10 September   Napoleon prepares project for initial invasion force of 114,000 men and 7,000 horses.

19 October   Secret Franco-Spanish military alliance concluded.

1804

January   70,000 French troops encamped near Boulogne.

12 December   Spain declares war on Britain.

1805

18 January   Admiral Villeneuve, commander of the Combined Fleet, makes abortive attempt to leave Toulon.

30 March   Villeneuve sails from Toulon for Martinique.

4 April   Nelson learns of Villeneuve's escape from Toulon.

10 April   Villeneuve, with Gravina's squadron, sails from Cadiz for Martinique.

11 April   Britain and Russia conclude an alliance against France.

12 May   Nelson leaves Portuguese waters for the West Indies, in pursuit of the Combined Fleet.

16 May   Villeneuve's fleet reaches Fort de France, Martinique.

June   Collingwood ordered south from England, ultimately to Cadiz.

4 June   Nelson arrives at Carlisle Bay, Barbados.

7 June   Villeneuve learns of Nelson's arrival in the West Indies.

16 June   Nelson learns of Villeneuve's departure for Europe.

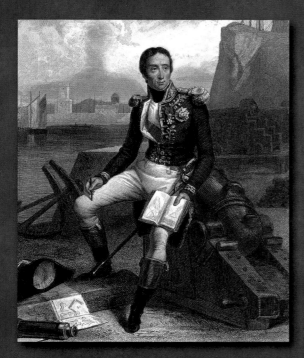

Admiral Eustace de Bruix (1759–1805). Bruix became a captain in the first year of the war with Britain (1793) and rose rapidly, becoming a rear-admiral four years later and serving as Minister of the Marine in 1798–99. Promoted to vice-admiral in 1799, he commanded the fleet at Rochefort until 1803, when he was appointed commander-in-chief of the invasion flotilla. He died in March 1805, seven months before Trafalgar. (Author's collection)

OPPOSITE Spanish sea-sailor. Much of a crew consisted of soldiers who had little or no experience of life – much less fighting – aboard ship, with adverse consequences for the efficiency of the otherwise impressively armed Spanish line of battle ships. (Umhey Collection)

BELOW Trafalgar: the situation at 1430hrs. The once slightly ragged and concave Franco-Spanish line has long since broken up into a mass of vessels fighting singly or in small groups. (Royal Naval Museum)

17 July	Admiral Allemand's squadron escapes from Rochefort.
22 July	Sir Robert Calder's force clashes indecisively with the Combined Fleet off Ferrol.
27 July	Villeneuve puts into Vigo Bay, on the north-west coast of Spain.
31 July	Villeneuve leaves Vigo for Ferrol, arriving two days later.
9 August	Austria formally joins Britain and Russia in the Third Coalition against France.
11 August	Combined Fleet sails south for Cadiz.
18 August	Nelson reaches Portsmouth and begins short stay in Britain.
26 August	*Grande Armée* at Boulogne breaks camp and marches for the Rhine.
15 September	Nelson sails from Portsmouth to join Collingwood's force off Cadiz.
28 September	Nelson assumes command of the Mediterranean Fleet.
19 October	First French ships leave Cadiz; Nelson orders pursuit.
20 October	Remainder of Combined Fleet leaves Cadiz.
21 October	Battle of Trafalgar.
22–29 October	Violent storms destroy nine ships captured at Trafalgar.
4 November	Off Cape Ortegal, south-west Spain, Sir Richard Strachan captures four ships which had escaped from Trafalgar.

DESIGN AND DEVELOPMENT

Between the 16th century and the 18th century maritime fighting vessels all shared the same essential elements: all were constructed from timber, all were powered by canvas sails, all were controlled by ropes or 'lines' made from hemp or similar material, and all employed anchors of similar design and function. Men of war and their successors all had a three-masted rig with square sails, each performing so as to make maximum use of the wind, reduce human effort, and to enable operation of the ship under changing conditions. Naval guns were all smoothbore muzzle loaders, initially cast from bronze though, by Trafalgar, from iron. All men of war and, later, ships of the line, were of a sufficient structural strength to mount large guns and to absorb much of the intense gunfire produced by similar enemy ships.

The ships of the line that fought at Trafalgar were direct descendants of the great men of war that had fought in the three Anglo-Dutch wars of the mid and late 17th century. In turn the men of war were themselves the product of innovations to the English and Spanish galleons that had fought one another in the 16th century during the reigns of Elizabeth I (r.1558–1603) and Philip II (r.1556–98) of Spain. Such vessels, particularly those of Spain, were massive floating fortresses that relied more on concentrated firepower and less on closing with the enemy and boarding his vessels, as would eventually become more commonplace in naval combat in the 18th century. The battles fought between the English and the Spanish Armada in July 1588 resulted in few Spanish losses as a result of gunfire; in fact, subsequent storms accounted for much of the Armada's travails. Guns had yet to reach their full destructive potential and naval engineering had not

BRITISH SHIPS OF THE LINE AT TRAFALGAR – DATE LAUNCHED, NAME AND NUMBER OF GUNS

1762	Britannia (100)	1793	Minotaur (74); Spartiate (74) captured from the French in 1798; Belleisle (74); formerly the Formidable; captured from the French in 1795
1763	Defence (74)		
1765	Victory (100)		
1781	Africa (64); Agamemnon (64)		
1782	Polyphemus (64)	1794	Mars (74)
1783	Defiance (74); Thunderer (74)	1797	Neptune (98)
1786	Bellerophon (74)	1798	Téméraire (98); Ajax (74); Achille (74)
1787	Orion (74); Royal Sovereign (100)	1800	Conqueror (74)
1788	Prince (98)	1801	Dreadnought (98)
1789	Leviathan (74)	1803	Colossus (74)
1792	Tonnant (80); captured from the French in 1798	1804	Swiftsure (74)
		1805	Revenge (74)

advanced sufficiently to enable fleets to be manoeuvred in battle with any degree of precision or timeliness.

By the end of the 16th century, all major European states with access to the sea had created navies of one kind or another, but only the great maritime powers on the Atlantic seaboard – England, France, Spain and Holland – had built large warships for purposes of securing control of the sea through the deployment of a superior battle fleet. Such a force could either be deployed to confront and defeat the enemy in battle or at least keep it secure in port through blockade. Technological developments in western European navies shared much in common and, hence, one may identify trends in construction and design in one of the principal maritime nations to illustrate parallel developments in another. English (from 1707, with the Union of England and Scotland, British) ship-building well suits this exercise. The commissioning in England of the *Prince Royal*, the largest ship of the time, in 1610, perhaps inadvertently set the precedent for the construction of more three-deckers, which were impressively armed and ornately decorated, but difficult to manoeuvre. Further behemoths followed in the reign of James I (r.1603–25), such as the *Sovereign of the Seas*, which displaced 1,500 tons. James's son, Charles I (r.1625–49), sought to assemble a fleet of massive ships with firepower their principal feature, as opposed to more lightly armed commerce raiders.

The battle of La Hogue, 22–24 May 1692, one of four fleet actions fought in the War of the English Succession, inaugurating a long period of Anglo-French rivalry which did not come to a proper close until 1815.
(Author's collection)

HMS *VICTORY*

1. Spanker or driver
2. Mizzen topsail
3. Mizzen topgallant
4. Main course (or main sail)
5. Main topsail
6. Main topgallant
7. Main staysail
8. Main topmast staysail
9. Middle staysail
10. Fore course
11. Fore topsail
12. Fore topgallant
13. Jib
14. Flying jib
15. Waterline
16. Keel
17. Rudder
18. Admiral's cabin
19. Captain's cabin
20. White ensign

SPECIFICATIONS

Number of guns	100	Depth in hold	21ft 6in.
Length of the range of the gun deck	184ft	Tons burthen	2,162.53 tons
Length of keel for tonnage	152ft 7in.	Draught afore	23ft
Extreme breadth	51ft 10in.	Draught abaft	24ft

REDOUTABLE

Similar in appearance to *Victory*, save for having one less gundeck, the *Redoutable* was the most distinguished French ship at Trafalgar. A two-decker of 74 guns, she was built at Brest in 1790 and launched the following year. Of her crew of 643 she suffered, between the battle and the subsequent storm, an astonishingly high casualty rate of 88 per cent, of whom 75 per cent were killed or drowned.

SPECIFICATIONS

Length on the range of the gun deck	182ft 6in.	Tons burthen	1,929 tons
Length of keel for tonnage	157ft (estimated)	Draught afore	22ft
Extreme breadth	49ft	Draught abaft	23ft
Depth in hold	21ft 6in.		

Impressive though such vessels appeared, in operational terms they were ponderous, difficult to turn and armed with guns that required considerable time, effort and manpower to load – so many men, in fact, that ships could only fight with one broadside at a time. This limitation led to the allocation of more men to the guns and fewer to the sails and use of small arms, so ships tended to remain in position when fighting. Moreover, the days of the 'line of battle' – the formation by which ships followed in the wake of the next ahead, bow to stern, in order to make the best use of their firepower – was still not yet fully realized.

The three Anglo-Dutch Wars of the 17th century did much to alter naval fighting tactics and ship design. The United Netherlands (Holland) was the leading maritime power of its day, and by the time war began with England in 1652, tactical doctrine had begun to emphasize the broadside, with captains seeking to achieve the highest rate of fire possible. This was all very well if ships were concentrated and so disposed as to make the best use of their guns. Yet in the initial actions of the First Anglo-Dutch War, the potential power of the fleet was dissipated by the fact that it was divided into several squadrons, each forming its own line rather than concentrating as a single force. From 1653, however, when army generals assumed command, the principles of land warfare were applied to the sea on the theory – quickly shown to be correct – that greater effectiveness could be achieved if an admiral deployed all his available ships into a single continuous line. Thus was born that most famous of dispositions of the age of fighting sail – the line of battle – which, when employed at the two-day battle of the Gabbard in 1653, the English achieved so decisive a victory as to bring the war to a swift conclusion. Thereafter, line of battle became the standard method of fleet deployment; indeed, this orthodoxy would go virtually unchallenged until the end of the 18th century.

During the reign of Charles II (r.1660–85), England fought two further wars with Holland, though in both instances with indecisive results. During the second conflict, between 1664 and 1667, the poor results achieved by the English in battle may be attributed to the improvements in Dutch ship design and tactics implemented since the first war. Clearly, the English had not yet reached anything close to naval mastery, for in 1667 they did not assemble a powerful fleet, and thus were utterly unprepared when the Dutch boldly penetrated the River Medway, inflicted considerable damage to dockyards and houses and, most humiliatingly of all, captured the English flagship, *Royal Charles*. During the Third Anglo-Dutch War, from 1672 to 1674, again only the largest ships took part in fleet engagements, with line of battle now firmly established as the standard formation.

Notwithstanding the lacklustre results of this indecisive conflict, Charles II carried on with the shipbuilding programme begun during Cromwell's reign and the ship of the line underwent further and positive change. The English were not alone; French and Spanish also built several three-decker ships of 100 guns or more, plus numerous others boasting lesser armament, such as the two-decked 70-gun ship of the line, which became the mainstay of the English fleet. The new enthusiasm for such vessels was exemplified by the fact that, in a single year, 1677, English dockyards produced thirty new ships of the line. The notion of using ships of the line had reached a mature

A gun protruding through a port in a ship of the line. Ships of the line had to operate as floating gun platforms, their principal function being to batter the enemy into submission with weapons such as that shown here mounted on the ship's broadside. (Philip Haythornthwaite)

state and hereafter this category of heavily-armed, square-rigged, three-masted vessels would constitute the backbone of all great European navies.

Nothing contributed more to the rise of the great fighting ships of the late 17th century than the long phase of Anglo-French rivalry that began as soon as William III came to power in England in 1689. England now confronted a new, much more powerful rival (on land, in any event) than Holland – France, under Louis XIV (r.1643–1715). During the extended period of the conflict between them (despite a hiatus from 1697 to 1702, the war did not end until 1714), the ship of the line was supreme upon the seas, with the balance favouring France between 1689 and 1697, partly as a result of Louis having constructed a large fleet capable of defeating the combined efforts of the English and Dutch, as at Beachy Head in June 1690. During this period French and English ships were rather different in design, the former

SPANISH SHIPS AT TRAFALGAR – DATE LAUNCHED, NAME AND NUMBER OF GUNS

1749	*Rayo* (100)	1785	*San Ildefonso* (74)
1766	*San Juan Nepomuceno* (74)	1787	*San Leandro* (64)
1767	*San Francisco de Asís* (74)	1794	*Monarca* (74); *Montañes* (74); *Principe*
1768	*San Agustín* (74)		*de Asturias* (112)
1769	*Santísima Trinidad* (136)	1795	*Neptuno* (72)
1779	*San Justo* (74)	1798	*Argonauta* (80)
1784	*Santa Ana* (112); *Bahama* (74)		

sporting a more angular stern and quarters, and being more rounded in the bows. But it was the inexperience of the English crews rather than any deficiency in ship design which accounted for their defeat on this occasion. Still, Beachy Head would mark the last time the English would lose a fleet engagement against their hereditary enemies, and only two years later, first at Barfleur and then at La Hogue, much of the French fleet was sunk or captured. Thereafter, the French navy would never

French ship of the line under construction. French designs were so much admired by their enemies that captured vessels were regularly copied by British shipwrights and officials at the Admiralty. (Terry Crowdy)

again outnumber the English, and the war ended in 1697 after the French demonstrated great skill at commerce raiding as an alternative to pitched battles involving ships of the line.

Perhaps France could never have outfought Britain at sea, since geography favoured the latter with respect to maritime matters. Being an island, Britain self-evidently depended for its defence upon its strength on the waves, while the navy also served the secondary – but by no means unimportant – role of defending merchant vessels, trade routes and colonies. France, on the other hand, though she too depended on the sea and had a very lengthy coastline with several excellent deep-water ports, possessed a vulnerable land frontier to the north and north-east, and thus necessarily required a sizeable army. This inescapable fact, combined with Louis' expansionist policies, meant that although France was considerably larger than Britain both geographically and demographically, her resources were disproportionately allocated to her land forces, whereas Britain, secure from attack by land, did precisely the opposite. As a result, for the first half of the 18th century the French would pose nothing like the significant naval threat to Britain that she would in the second half.

As a result, during the War of the Spanish Succession (1702–14), during the reign of Queen Anne (r.1702–14), the Royal Navy, deploying large fleets of ships of the line, was able to play a crucial part in the captures of such strategically important points in the Mediterranean as Gibraltar and Minorca. The French foolishly did not

FRENCH SHIPS AT TRAFALGAR – DATE LAUNCHED, NAME AND NUMBER OF GUNS

1775	Berwick (74); originally British, captured by the French in 1795	1796	Duguay-Trouin (74)
		1798	Aigle (74)
1784	Fougueux (74)	1799	Intrépide (74)
1787	Swiftsure (74)	1801	Scipion (74)
1789	Mont Blanc (74); Indomptable (80)	1803	Bucentaure (80); Neptune (80);
1790	Redoutable (74)		Achille (74)
1794	Formidable (80); Argonaute (74)	1804	Algésiras (74)
1795	Héros (74)	1805	Pluton (74)

prepare a large battle fleet, as a result of which in the five major actions of the war, they either failed to achieve their objective or suffered a tactical defeat. With no major naval threat to hand, therefore, the responsibility of the several British fleets deployed during the war was to seek out and destroy privateers, a task carried out with reasonable success, as well as to convey troops across the seas to seize French colonial possessions.

By the end of the war in 1714 the Royal Navy had emerged as a permanent institution of the nation. The fleet exceeded 200 vessels of all types. However, ship design largely stood static for the next generation owing to institutional conservatism. A strict adherence to standard dimensions in shipbuilding suppressed innovation, as did the retention of ineffective types, such as the 80-gun ship. The orthodox tactics of the times laid out in the Admiralty's *Fighting Instructions* discouraged any tactical initiative by commanding officers.

In the period up through the mid 18th century, the British Empire continued to expand, thus requiring the navy to defend the merchant vessels that supplied colonial possessions in North America, the West Indies, India and elsewhere. Trade connected with these territories was lucrative, but the great distances from the mother country left it vulnerable to interception. The French fully appreciated this weakness and consequently constructed a new fleet after the War of the Spanish Succession. The classic 74-gun ship, a two-decker, resulted from this programme of naval expansion, and was to prove itself a highly effective fighting vessel, particularly after mid century, for it was large enough to stand in the line of battle yet less expensive than the old 100-gun ship, which mounted ordnance on three decks and took longer to build.

Yet it was not France against which Britain's growing naval might would be pitted in the decades immediately following the death of Louis XIV, but Spain – the third greatest maritime power. In the short-term conflicts fought between 1718 and 1727, and in a considerably longer one known as the War of Jenkins' Ear which began in 1739, British operations extended over great distances, with fighting conducted in the waters of Spain's New World empire, along the Spanish coast itself and against the enemy's colonies as far as the distant Pacific. Ship design largely stagnated during this period, not least because the French failed to place great emphasis on a substantial battle fleet during the wars of Louis XIV, and because for Britain, the quarter century from 1714 to 1739 had been largely peaceful; with Spain easily beaten in two minor conflicts and with no major British naval defeat since 1690, there existed no obvious motive to alter ship design. The chief innovation was that the major European navies began to standardize the basic profile and structure of the ship of the line in terms of the types of guns it carried, the weight of their shot, and the dimensions of the ship's hull and decks.

The struggle against France was renewed in 1744, by which time Louis XV possessed a very respectable navy, though his attempts to support a projected invasion of Britain were ruined at the end of February by a storm that caused severe damage to the French fleet. The context of this event – the War of the Austrian Succession (1740–48), fought partly at sea – demonstrated Britain's growing naval dominance,

REAR-ADMIRAL CHARLES MAGON

Charles Magon is shown here mortally wounded at Trafalgar. Known for his violent temper and recklessness, Magon might perhaps have made a better – certainly a more daring – commander of the French fleet than Villeneuve and might have fared better off Cape Finisterre against Sir Robert Calder after the return of the Combined Fleet from the West Indies.

Born in Brittany in 1763 into an aristocratic family, Magon entered the navy as a boy and saw his first combat as an *aspirante* (midshipman) at the age of 14 during the battle of Ushant in December 1781. In the same year he served in the West Indies where he took part in Admiral de Guichen's inconclusive actions against Admiral Rodney off Martinique. As a result of severe damage to Magon's ship, the *Caton*, which required repairs, Magon was not present when Rodney defeated de Grasse at Les Saintes in April 1782. Later in the campaign, however, the *Caton* was captured and Magon was taken prisoner.

He served as a captain in Philippine waters and escorted home two East Indiamen carrying valuable cargo, for which efforts he was awarded an ornamental belt by an organization of merchants. At Trafalgar, Magon displayed the belt, inlaid with silver, on the quarterdeck and offered it as a prize to the first man who would board

the enemy. In 1804, Magon, then a rear-admiral, was appointed command of the advanced guard of gunboats which were assigned to lead the invasion flotilla in the projected descent on the coast of England.

In April 1805, Magon was ordered to the West Indies with two ships of the line and a convoy of troops to reinforce Villeneuve. He reached Martinique in early June and served in the action against Calder off Finisterre on 22 July during Villeneuve's return to European waters. On seeing Villeneuve's signal to call off the action, Magon threw his wig and telescope overboard in a fit of rage and screamed epithets at Villeneuve's ship as it passed.

Magon was third in command at Trafalgar, at which he served aboard the *Algésiras* (74). In the late afternoon his ship fouled two enemy ships and was raked by the *Tonnant* (80). In the process of assembling a boarding party Magon was struck in rapid succession by three musket balls, the first of which carried away his hat and wig, the second struck his right arm, and the third lodged in his shoulder. Notwithstanding intense pain and severe blood loss, Magon remained standing on his quarterdeck preparing his men to board. But it was not to be: moments later he was killed instantly by a splinter or round shot, which struck him in the stomach. (Author's collection)

not least as a result of its victory at Finisterre in May 1747. Partly as a result of the loss of so many of its ships, France agreed to peace the following year and began a building programme of 74-gun ships to replace some of the older types. At about the same time, British admirals began to deviate from the rigid *Fighting Instructions* and adopt more aggressive tactics that did not confine commanders to the mere inconclusive slogging matches which normally took place between two opposing lines sailing on parallel courses. The French and Spanish did not follow suit and continued to deploy their fleets in orthodox line of battle formation.

During the next conflict with France, the Seven Years' War (1756–63), Britain achieved unprecedented gains on both land and sea, with the navy playing a prominent part in the conquest of Canada and the French possessions in India, as well as in several significant engagements at sea – above all the fleet action at Quiberon Bay in Brittany – so that by war's end the Royal Navy emerged with an enhanced reputation for accomplished seamanship, high morale and a respectable standard of gunnery. Britain remained at peace for more than a decade before the rebellious American colonies obliged her to dispatch large numbers of troops across the Atlantic to fight in the War of American Independence (1775–83). As the colonists possessed no fleet – and even on establishing a navy the infant United States could put to sea only small vessels and privateers – the Royal Navy played little part in the initial years of the conflict except in conveying military expeditions to coastal cities like Charleston and New York and reinforcing the Canadian theatre. When, however, in 1778 France joined the rebels' side, the Royal Navy faced a substantial foe, soon thereafter joined by Spain and Holland. With no allies of her own, Britain found herself opposed by her principal continental rival – one that could concentrate its naval resources without the distraction of having to wage a land campaign in Europe. Between them, France, Spain and Holland mustered more ships of the line than Britain – the first time in the 18th century that numerical superiority was achieved over the Royal Navy – though these three powers never actually cooperated usefully enough to take full advantage of this superiority. Most of the naval battles of the conflict were in fact fought in the West Indies from 1780, the final and decisive encounter – very much in Britain's favour – occurring at The Saintes in April 1782, though ships of the line played a prominent part at the siege and relief of Gibraltar (1779–83), as well.

In an age of slow technological development – at least in naval terms – one innovation played an important part in the conflict, for in 1779 the British, alone, introduced the idea of coppering ships' bottoms. The nailing of sheets of copper to the underside of a ship's hull was meant to remedy the problem of shipworm in the tropics and the growth of marine life – both vegetation and barnacles – in cooler climates, and to slow the process of rot generally. Various types of worm attacked a ship's planking below the waterline, boring their way through and eventually causing severe structural damage. Marine vegetation and parasitic crustaceans posed lesser threats, but merely by clinging on they affected the speed of the vessel unless regularly scraped or burned off in port, where the ship had to be radically heeled over to expose the surface well below the waterline. In time, most existing ships and those constructed after 1779 were coppered

as a standard component of the hull. Coppering was particularly advantageous in the West Indies, where British ships cruising those waters required much less maintenance, whereas the French had regularly to lay up vessels to dislodge their slimy and destructive passengers. Thus, increased speed and the ability of ships to remain at sea longer more than justified the considerable expense of coppering their bottoms.

The French and Spanish having briefly held the advantage in the Channel in 1780, Britain was not prepared to see the opportunity repeated, and undertook an impressive building programme of ships of the line. Thus, by the time the French Revolutionary Wars (1792–1802, Britain joining in 1793) began, the Royal Navy was second to none, possessing not only the largest number of ships in the world, but, as explained, superior (and exclusive) technology in the form of copper-bottomed hulls.

The 74 – the smallest ship considered powerful enough to serve in the line of battle – had become by this time the workhorse and mainstay of the major European navies, its efficacy shown in the major fleet actions of the era – the Glorious First of June (1794), St. Vincent (1797), the Nile (1798) and Copenhagen (1801) – and a host of smaller engagements. During this and the subsequent conflict known as the Napoleonic Wars (1803–15), in which Trafalgar took place, the navy would capitalize on its already high reputation by repeatedly defeating various opponents and enhancing that reputation to the highest point in its long history – much of it achieved with ships of the line whose principal characteristics had remained largely unchanged for more than a hundred years.

The battle of the Glorious First of June (1794), the first fleet action of the French Revolutionary Wars (1792–1802). Off Ushant, the superiority of British leadership, discipline, gunnery, and seamanship became apparent more than a decade before the climactic encounter at Trafalgar. (Author's collection)

TECHNICAL SPECIFICATIONS

THE RATING SYSTEM

The basic design of British, French and Spanish ships of the line was the same, though most British shipwrights admitted the superiority of French designs, a fact supported by the frequency with which British vessels were either copied after their French counterparts or were themselves captured French ships commissioned into the service of the Royal Navy after a minimum of alterations. A French 120-gun ship, the *Marseilles*, captured at Toulon in 1793, particularly impressed her captors, one of whom found her 'lines uncommonly fine' and considered her 'a good sea boat'. She also sailed remarkably well: 'notwithstanding her immense size,' he continued, 'she worked and sailed like a frigate.' Indeed, throughout the French Revolutionary and Napoleonic Wars, French ships were observed by British captains and crews to be faster and to steer more effectively. One British captain noted that 'the ships of France and Spain are generally superior to those of England, both in size, weight of metal and number of men, outsailing them in fleets, and often in single ships, carrying their guns higher out of the water, and in all other respects better found for the material of war'. Such opinions were by no means universal, but they had many advocates, who argued that the essential advantage of the French ship of the line lay in its size and dimensions. One British observer wrote:

> I am of the opinion that all the ships of the present navy are too short, from ten to thirty feet according to their rates. If ships in future were to be built so much longer as to admit of an additional timber between every port, and if the foremost and aftermost gunports

VICE-ADMIRAL CUTHBERT COLLINGWOOD

Born in Yorkshire in 1748, Collingwood was 57 at Trafalgar, a quiet, patriotic man who, quite unlike his much younger friend Nelson, sought no publicity or fame. Highly skilled in seamanship and already immensely experienced by the time of Trafalgar, he was known for his strict discipline, the high morale of the crews in his fleet, and the remarkable standard of the training of his men.

Collingwood joined the navy at the age of 11 with the aid of his maternal uncle, a captain in the service. He served first aboard the frigate *Shannon* before becoming 4th lieutenant of the *Somerset* (74) in 1775, having already served 14 years as a midshipman and master's mate. Collingwood was present in Boston Harbour during the battle of Bunker Hill in June 1775 and was later transferred for service in the West Indies under Admiral Sir Peter Parker. He commanded the frigate *Lowestoffe* (32), later the armed brig *Badger* and, with the rank of post captain, the *Hinchinbroke* (28).

Like Nelson, Collingwood served in the ill-fated expedition against the Spanish colony of Nicaragua, where nearly all of his shipmates succumbed to disease. At Jamaica he was assigned command of the frigate *Pelican*, which was shipwrecked in a hurricane on Morant Keys, where he and his crew were stranded for ten days before being rescued by the frigate *Diamond*. At the conclusion of the War of American Independence (1775–83), Collingwood came home, returning to sea upon the outbreak of war with Revolutionary France in 1793. A flag captain of the *Barfleur* (98) he fought at the Glorious First of June the following year, where he succeeded Rear-Admiral Bowyer when that officer was seriously wounded. Three years later, as captain of the *Excellent* (74) at the battle of St. Vincent, Collingwood earned for himself the King's gold medal for gallant conduct. He spent the next eight years on continuous blockade duty off various French and Spanish ports until, with the rank of vice-admiral, he came under Nelson's command shortly before Trafalgar, in which battle he led the lee column, consisting of 15 ships of the line, including his own flagship, the *Royal Sovereign* (100). On Nelson's death, Collingwood assumed command of the Mediterranean Fleet.

After Trafalgar Collingwood was raised to the peerage and remained at sea, serving off the Spanish coast and in the Mediterranean, where, aboard the *Ville de Paris* (100), he died in 1810, aged 62, as a result of poor health caused by severe fatigue and the constant anxiety connected with his duties, he having been home for only a single year in the whole course of the wars with France since 1793. Collingwood was buried near Nelson in St Paul's Cathedral. Collingwood's dispatch to the Admiralty following Trafalgar stands as one of the great documents of British naval history. Amidst his account of the action itself and Nelson's death he movingly wrote:

After such a Victory, it may appear unnecessary to enter into enconiums on the particular parts taken by the several Commanders; the conclusion says more on the subject than I have language to express; the spirit which animated all was the same: when all exert themselves zealously in the country's service, all deserve that their high merit should stand recorded; and never was high merit more conspicuous than in the battle I have described. (Author's collection) were placed a greater distance from the extremities, they would be stronger and safer, and have more room for fighting their guns.

Whatever their nationality, large vessels were divided into six different classes, or rates, according to the number of guns they carried. In the Royal Navy the system was known as 'rating'. Smaller vessels were designated as 'unrated'.

In the French navy ships of the line or *vaisseaux* consisted of ships mounting 118, 110, 80, and 74 guns, and those with between 54 and 74 guns. Of these, the 74 was the most numerous. Below these came frigates, corvettes and various other types of vessel. In the Spanish navy, ships of the line carried 120, 112, 94, 74–80, 64–68, 58–64, and 50 guns, with those mounting 74–80 guns being by far the most numerous. As with the French, the only other rating – if indeed the term can be applied to such a large range of ship types – consisted of frigates, corvettes, xebecs and a host of lesser vessels.

Ships of the line in British service consisted only of the first three rates, in contrast to fourth rates of 50 to 60 guns, frigates, mounting 28 to 44 guns, classed as fifth rates and which, though present at Trafalgar, did not exchange fire there, sixth rate post ships mounting between 20 and 28 guns, and a host of unrated vessels including sloops, brigs and gunboats.

The ships of the line present at Trafalgar ranged in armament from the ubiquitous 74 to the massive, four-decked, 136-gun *Santísima Trinidad*. With the sole exception of that Spanish giant, the armament mounted on a ship of the line stood on two or three decks with the heaviest guns on the lowest deck and the lighter pieces placed progressively higher so as to prevent the ship from heeling over and capsizing. It is important to note that, in all three navies, this armament referred only to 'great' or 'long' guns – what today are commonly, though erroneously, called 'cannon', and therefore excluded carronades and howitzers, which will be described later.

The massive four-decker, *Santísima Trinidad*, built in the Spanish colonial dockyard at Havana in 1769 from American timber. Unlike the French and British, the Spanish constructed many of their principal ships in facilities overseas. (Umhey Collection)

FIRST RATES

First rates, like Horatio Nelson's flagship, the *Victory* and the *Royal Sovereign*, under Collingwood, the second-in-command, carried crews of between 823 (677 naval personnel and 146 Royal Marines) and 826 men (697 naval and 129 Royal Marines), respectively. These were massive structures, with three gun decks, carrying 32-pounder guns on the lower gun deck, 24-pounders on the middle deck, and 18- or 12-pounders on their upper gun deck and quarterdeck, supplemented with carronades.

A first rate carried 100 to 120 guns, with the weight of both broadsides totalling approximately 2,500lb of iron shot.

A first rate was ponderous in the water by the standards of its smaller consorts, with an average speed of 7 to 8 knots. It bore the admiral of the fleet, who occupied the cabin aft. Not surprisingly, a first rate required a prodigious amount of timber to construct – approximately 300,000 cubic feet, 90 per cent of which was oak – the equivalent of about 6,000 trees, extracted from approximately 100 acres of woodland. Materials on this scale, and the cost of maintaining these vessels, meant that first rates were exceedingly expensive to build, and hence there were only ten in the Royal Navy at the end of 1803, with three more under construction. In 1805, the French had five first rates, though none of these was present at Trafalgar. In the same year the Spanish possessed seven, of which four fought in the battle, these being: *Rayo* (100), with a crew of 830 men and her guns arrayed as follows: 30 × 36-pounders on her lower deck, 32 × 24-pounders on her middle deck, 30 × 18-pounders on her upper deck, 6 × 8-pounders on her quarterdeck, and 2 × 8-pounders on her forecastle; *Santísima Trinidad* (136), with a crew of 1,048 (604 naval, 382 infantry, 62 marine artillery); *Santa Ana* (112); and the *Príncipe de Asturias* (112), with a ship's company of 1,189. The British had three first rates at Trafalgar, *Britannia*, of 100 guns, being the third.

SECOND RATES

Second rates in the Royal Navy, like their larger counterparts, also carried guns on three decks, though being slightly smaller than the largest class of ship of the line, their armament numbered slightly fewer, with 90 to 98 guns: 32-pounders on the lower gun deck, 18-pounders on the middle gun deck and 12-pounders on the upper gun deck and quarterdeck, with a weight of both broadsides of approximately 2,300lb. The *Téméraire*, *Neptune*, *Dreadnought* and *Prince* all mounted 98 guns. Being armed with fewer guns, second rates carried a proportionally smaller crew of about 750 men. As with first rates, these ships could also be used as flagships. Neither the French nor the Spanish possessed equivalent vessels to the British second rate at Trafalgar.

THIRD RATES

Third rates of the Royal Navy carried between 74 and 84 guns on two decks and were the most common vessel to fight in the line of battle. When the Trafalgar campaign began, the British had 152 third rates, of which nine were 80 or 84-gun ships, 96 had 74 guns each and 36 carried 64 guns. As discussed, the most numerous and most effective of these was the 74, which carried 24- or 36-pounder guns on the lower gun deck, 24- or 18-pounder guns on the upper deck and 9- or 12-pounder guns on the quarterdeck, with a weight of both broadsides of about 1,764lb. A British third rate, depending on class and armament, carried a crew of between 550 and 700. A typical 74 in British service measured about 170 feet in length on the lower gun deck, 48 feet in breadth, displaced 1,670 tons and had a draught of 20 to 22 feet. A 74, running before the wind, could reach a speed of 11 knots. Constructing a 74-gun ship required about 120,500 cubic feet of timber, the equivalent of about 2,400 full-grown oaks, drawn from about 70 acres of woodland, though some of this bulk was reduced once the wood had been cut and shaped for use. Third rates were occasionally employed as flagships, but they normally served as the ordinary fighting machine of a battle fleet or, owing to their smaller size, on detached service with independent squadrons, accompanied by frigates. Nelson had 19 third rates at Trafalgar, all 74s apart from the 80-gun *Tonnant* and three 64s.

All of the French ships of the line at Trafalgar were third rates, consisting of two-deckers mounting 74 or 80 guns, of which Pierre de Villeneuve had 14 of the former and four of the latter, including such vessels as the *Mont Blanc*, with a crew of 755 (495 sailors, 215 infantry, and 45 marine artillery) and the *Fougueux*, with 755 men. But it is the famous *Redoutable* (74) which most concerns us here. Her armament was mounted as follows: 28 x 36-pounders on her lower deck, 30 x 24-pounders on her upper deck, 12 x 8-pounders on her quarterdeck, and 4 x 8-pounders on her forecastle. Her poop carried four or six 36-pdr howitzers, though these, like the carronades in British service, were not included when calculating her rating. *Redoutable*'s single broadside weight totalled 890lb, or 988 including her howitzers. Her crew numbered 643: 403 naval personnel, 200 infantry, and 40 marine artillerists. *Redoutable* was designed by the noted naval architect Jacques Noël Sane, laid down at Brest in January 1790 and launched as the *Suffren* (after the distinguished admiral) in May 1791, but renamed *Redoutable* in May 1794.

The Spanish had 11 third rates at Trafalgar, one of 80 guns (*Neptuno*), nine carrying 74 guns, and one mounting 64 guns (*San Leandro*). Typical complements for Spanish 74s included that of the *Bahama*, with 690 men, and the *San Francisco de Asís*, with a crew of 657.

A French ship of the line. The French built four types of ship of the line, consisting of 120- and 110-gun three-deckers, and 80- and 74-gun two-deckers, with the 80 designed to be faster and more powerful than the British 74. A French 74, the typical workhorse shown here, carried about 750 officers and men. (Author's collection)

HMS *VICTORY* VIEWED FROM ABOVE

1. Mizzen boom
2. Signal-flag lockers
3. Mizzenmast
4. Hammock netting
5. Poop deck
6. Admiral Lord Nelson's cabin
7. Captain Hardy's cabin
8. Copper sheathing
9. Entry port and side steps
10. Compass and hourglass

11. Ship's wheel
12. Quarterdeck
13. Spot where Nelson fell
14. Ladderway
15. Main mast
16. Upper gun deck (12-pounder guns)
17. Middle gun deck (24-pounder guns)
18. Lower gun deck (32-pounder guns)
19. Main hatchway
20. Ship's boats

21. Belfry
22. Forecastle
23. Stem
24. Marines' catwalk
25. Cathead
26. Anchor
27. Bowsprit
28. Figurehead
29. Mizzen shrouds
30. Main shrouds
31. Fore shrouds
32. 68-pounder carronades
33. Gun ports

Complex though the ship of the line appeared with its miles of rigging and its numerous (not to mention voluminous) sails, it was in essence a floating gun platform on a grand scale, with its massive armament arrayed along its broadside – that is to say, along the length of the ship on both sides – this being the most efficient manner of deploying its armoury and the only practical method of arranging its guns if the ship was to remain afloat. This configuration suffered from the single, though not insignificant disadvantage that it left both bow and stern highly vulnerable to enemy fire, for not only was a ship of the line incapable of mounting guns in any meaningful numbers either facing forward or aft; the ship was also structurally weakest precisely at these two points, particularly the utterly defenceless windows of the captain's cabin at the rear of the vessel.

While they fall outside the focus of this study, frigates were present at Trafalgar and played an important supporting role to ships of the line. Although frigates did not fight in fleet actions – they were incapable of standing up to the tremendous firepower of their larger consorts – they nevertheless performed a vital function as signallers, flying the admiral's instructions aloft in the form of a series of coloured flags whose meaning could be interpreted with a code book. They normally served in a reconnaissance role, seeking out the enemy's fleet, following its movements until battle could be joined. Frigates mounted between 28 and 44 guns on a single deck and carried a crew of approximately 250 men. Naval tradition stipulated that ships of the line were not to fire on frigates unless fired on first – a rare occurrence, indeed; this was respected at Trafalgar, where the guns aboard both fleets' frigates remained silent.

SAILS AND RIGGING

To refer to a ship of the line merely as a floating gun platform – or perhaps more accurately, two or three platforms in a single craft – is somewhat inaccurate, for its armament was useless unless the vessel itself could not merely be brought into the enemy's presence, but perform complex manoeuvres once engaged. Notwithstanding the impressive array of skills found aboard a ship of the line and the complexity of its design and construction, natural phenomena played a fundamental role in a crew's ability to control and sail their vessel, including wind speed and direction, the tides and the ocean's currents. Fleets simply could not be moved like armies, for though geographical, meteorological and other factors naturally limited the speed at which armies could move and influenced their line of march, naval forces suffered some forms of impediment not experienced on land.

Fleets, for instance, could be held up in port for days or even weeks at a time by adverse winds. Even when in the open sea a ship could not reach its destination merely by plotting a straight course; rather, an oblique approach was required to make best use of the wind. To the uninitiated, the sea appears open and free of obstacles; this is deceptive, and before the age of steam no mariner could direct his vessel with the same ease with which the crow flies directly from point to point. Under becalmed conditions a ship simply drifted aimlessly, the crew utterly powerless. Moreover, in the course of a journey a ship might encounter a hostile vessel or, more likely, heavy weather or even a storm, uncharted rocks or other hazards. Indeed, storms and accidents accounted for the vast majority of losses suffered by navies in the age of sail, not close action.

Ships of the line harnessed the power of the wind with the aid of complex rigging, including three vertical masts, spars, sails, ropes of seemingly interminable length and a massive array of other paraphernalia such as pulleys and blocks, all working together to propel the vessel in the most efficient manner possible. An enormous vocabulary existed to cover every feature of a ship, not least the sails, but also all its standing rigging (a series of ropes or 'lines' variously known as shrouds, stays, and backstays, which supported the masts) and running rigging (another set of ropes known as sheets, tacks, bowlines, braces, lifts and halliards, used to support and manipulate the sails). It was vital that 'topmen' – those who worked up the masts – possessed an intimate understanding of this terminology. Sails, for instance, were (in British parlance) secured or 'bent' to yards (or booms or gaffs), spread when 'making sail', furled when 'reducing sail' and, under stormy conditions, 'reefed', that is, reduced in area.

Made from strips of strong canvas of varying strength depending on their purpose, sails were nearly all 'square' – hence the term 'square-rigged' – suspended from yards and opened across the width of the vessel, a position known as athwartships. In reality most sails were in fact wider at the bottom than at the top and thus not genuinely square. Others could not be called 'square' at all, being 'lateen' – that is, triangular in shape, and considerably fewer in number. There were also 'fore-and-aft sails' that were suspended down the centreline of the ship. All of these various sails were assigned a particular name based on the type of mast or stay to which they were suspended by their position, and known to all sailors who worked above decks (plural, since there was no single upper deck running along the length of a ship of the line, but rather several, including the forecastle and poop). Every sail served a specific function and could be deployed into a veritable cloud of canvas, so enabling the captain to make best use of prevailing conditions.

MASTS AND SHROUDS

Ships of the line had three vertical masts, the central one being known as the mainmast. The foremast, as is implied, stood in the forwardmost position and the rearmost mast, known as the mizzenmast (or 'mizen' to contemporaries), stood aft. Despite appearances from a distance, a mast was not made from a single piece of timber, but rather consisted of several sections glued together, pinned with iron nails and bound with coils of rope or iron bands. The various sections were named according to their respective positions which, in ascending order, were the lower mast, topmast, topgallant mast and royalmast. The lower mast was secured deep in the ship's interior, and passed up through each deck, above which it was held in position by

32-POUNDER GUN CARRIAGE

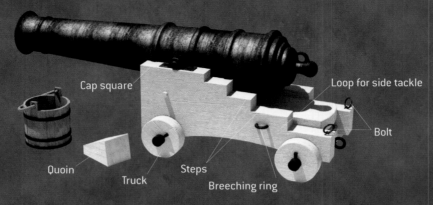

Cap square

Loop for side tackle

Bolt

Quoin

Truck

Steps

Breeching ring

LONG GUN – PLAN VIEW

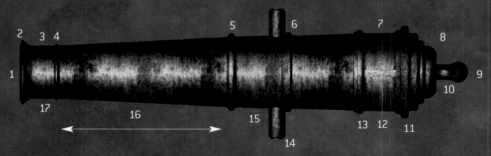

1. Face
2. Muzzle swell
3. Muzzle
4. Muzzle astragal
5. Second reinforce ring
6. First reinforce ring
7. First reinforce
8. Cascable
9. Button
10. Thimble
11. Base ring
12. Vent
13. Vent astragal
14. Trunnion
15. Second reinforce
16. Chase
17. Neck

CUTAWAY OF A LOADED GUN

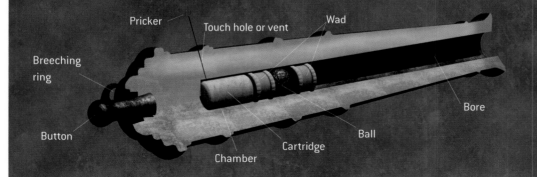

Pricker

Touch hole or vent

Wad

Breeching ring

Button

Chamber

Cartridge

Ball

Bore

forestays. These stretched from the masts along the centreline of the ship, while two sets of backstays extended to the rear of the ship, where they were secured.

The masts were further secured, this time athwartships, by shrouds, a series of thick lines (ropes) spliced so as to produce a triangular netting, wide at their base but gradually tapering as they rose above the decks to come to a point high up the mast. Shrouds played a critical part in supporting the masts laterally and formed a sort of ladder with the addition of horizontal ropes known as ratlines which seamen used to climb aloft to work on the masts, spars, sails or rigging. The shrouds terminated at a wooden platform (known as a top) attached to each vertical mast, and on this sailors could perform work or issue fire during battle. Another set of smaller shrouds, fastened to the tops and extending upwards, enabled a sailor to ascend even higher into the rigging. Once he reached the desired point aloft he could move across yards by keeping a foothold on one of a series of rope stirrups, known as a horse, and gripping the yard under his arms.

Extending forward from the bow at an angle of up to 25 degrees was the bowsprit, which served to support a series of triangular sails including the jib, flying jib, foretopmast staysail, and fore staysail. Masts were usually made of pine, while hemp was the principal material used in the manufacture of rope, which, if stood end to end, measured several miles. Not only had the masts and spars to be stout enough to make best use of the wind, they had also to bear up to the punishment of severe weather and enemy fire.

Launching a ship of the line. Vessels of this size took years to build and months to fit out with masts, sails, guns, equipment and stores. This type of ship was the single most complex, sophisticated and expensive piece of technology of its day, requiring not only hundreds of skilled men to sail and maintain it, but a whole network of supporting institutions to keep it operational. (Royal Naval Museum)

YARDS

Yards consisted of long pieces of cylindrical timber, generally fashioned from fir, suspended at intervals up the mast so that sails could be extended along them, unfurled, and so deployed as to fill with wind and thus propel the ship. Most yards were fixed at right angles to the mast, though some were hung obliquely as needed. The size of a yard was proportionate to the size of the mast to which it was affixed and the dimensions of the sail it supported. Like the masts, the larger yards were fashioned from several pieces of timber, the centre section being of a uniform thickness but the exterior joints tapering to a point as they extended out. Yards were held in place by a complex series of ropes and pulleys, but their angle could be adjusted as required. To deploy the multiplicity of sails, sailors used the horses that hung down from every yard to support themselves as they worked. Each horse passed through an eye tied at the base of each stirrup, thus enabling sailors to walk along the yard to furl, reef or bend a sail – all hazardous tasks and not the realm of the faint-hearted. Men who through clumsiness or vertigo fell overboard stood some chance of survival, whereas those who struck the deck were almost invariably killed.

NAVAL ARMAMENT

'LONG' OR 'GREAT' GUNS

The ship of the line was designed to fight in the line of battle – hence its alternative cognomen, 'line of battle ship' – employing the guns mounted on its broadsides to overpower opposing vessels, usually of squadron or fleet strength. Naval ordnance was of a very rudimentary design, consisting of a simple, cast-iron smoothbore tube mounted on a heavy carriage resting on fixed axles and fitted with four small wooden wheels called trucks. The carriage was made from elm, which could withstand shock better than oak – an essential feature so that the various bolts, eyes and ringbolts driven into the carriage to accommodate the rope fastenings did not split the wood. Moreover, if struck by a round shot, elm was less likely to splinter into fragments. The trucks themselves were also of elm, but of a solid piece cut horizontally from the trunk of a tree. To reduce its weight, the carriage was made with the minimum amount of wood and fittings required to support the barrel, yet at the same time remaining strong enough to withstand the considerable force of recoil generated when the gun was fired.

Specifically, the carriage had to withstand far more stress than the mere weight of the barrel; in particular, the carriage was so designed that the energy released on discharge was directed towards the rear axletree to prevent the gun from overturning. Without its restraining ropes and tackles, a 32-pounder gun could recoil 40–50ft across the deck, crushing everything in its wake – hence the importance of controlling it. To reduce the effect of recoil, guns were often restrained by a heavy cord, known as a breeching rope, fastened around the breech (rear) of the gun, down through a ring on each side of the carriage and finally fixed to two ring-bolts driven into the ship's side. This was but one method, favoured in the British service; the same effect, preferred by the French and Spanish, could be achieved by affixing a heavy rope to the sides of the carriage. However secured, sturdiness was essential in a breeching rope, for a force of 12 tons or more was exerted against it when the gun recoiled. Breeching ropes were measured out at three times the length of the gun barrel so that the weapon recoiled far enough to allow reloading through the muzzle. There were also two side tackles to enable the gun crew to run the gun forward through the port before firing. Finally, fitted between the rear of the gun carriage and the deck at the centreline was a train tackle, used to move the carriage backwards.

CARRONADES

The carronade, confined to use in the navies of Britain and the United States (the French and Spanish had howitzers, which were altogether different), was introduced into the service of the Royal Navy in 1779. Invented by General Robert Melville in 1752 and named for the Carron Iron Founding and Shipping Company near Glasgow, the carronade differed from the conventional gun as a consequence of its shorter and lighter barrel and its different method of mounting. While it had a shorter range, the carronade possessed several advantages over standard guns, especially its ability to fire a much heavier weight of shot – a massive 68lb ball being the largest – in proportion to the weight of the gun. It was also much more economical in terms of the expenditure of powder, for the proportion of gunpowder charge was much smaller than the weight of the shot. Aiming was considerably easier as well, since most carronades were mounted on a slide carriage, which absorbed most of the recoil and thus gunners expended much less effort re-siting the weapon for the next discharge. The carriage itself was mounted on a fixed block at the muzzle end of the weapon and on transverse casters at the breech end, thus enabling the gun to be rotated in numerous angled positions not easily achieved, or altogether impossible, by standard guns.

The carronade fired a hollow round shot at both a lower (i.e. flatter) trajectory and a lower velocity than a standard gun, as well as over a shorter distance, inflicting considerably greater damage since, rather than penetrating the hull like a solid iron ball, it broke up on impact, causing timber to shatter into clouds of deadly splinters. Alternatively, when loaded with specialized forms of anti-personnel ammunition such as grape shot or canister shot, the carronade unleashed an exceedingly lethal discharge at the crews manning the upper decks of an opposing vessel. It could also be elevated more than an ordinary gun and required fewer men to operate it. In short, practically its only shortcoming was its short range.

AMMUNITION

Naval ammunition aboard ships of the line varied little between European navies, but consisted predominantly of solid iron shot weighing 36, 24, 18, 12 or 8lb though both the French and Spanish system of weights was not the exact equivalent of their enemy's: thus, the equivalent of a British 36lb shot in the French service actually weighed 38lb 14oz. As French crews were generally less well trained and experienced than their British counterparts, they preferred disabling over round shot, the latter of which required considerable skill to be fired with accuracy at any but the closest distances. Disabling shot consisted of: bar shot – two halves of a small-calibre round shot joined together by a bar; grape or canister shot – musket balls encased in a tin, bottle or other container, that broke open on emerging from the mouth of the gun, spreading its contents like a giant shotgun; chain shot – two halves of a small round shot joined by a short link of chain; expanding shot – steel blades fixed together in a cluster and housed in a hollow sphere that opened in flight to sever lines and sails; and various other forms of ammunition meant to cut or tangle rigging and cause havoc amongst the enemy crew. French guns were standardized, like the ship types, in 1786, to prevent the confusion that hitherto arose from the manufacture of ordnance of unconventional calibres and the construction of ships of a multiplicity of designs and dimensions. The French had no carronades at Trafalgar, using in their stead the 36-pounder bronze *obusier de vaisseau* (naval howitzer), mounted on a carronade-style slide but resembling a howitzer and firing (at high angle) shells instead of solid shot; they exploded on or over the target by means of a timed fuse.

The traditional French gunnery tactic was to fire during the upward roll of the ship in order to damage an opponent's rigging, thus allowing commanders the option either to disengage from battle without risk of pursuit by their opponent or to disable the enemy sufficiently during a chase as to hinder his movements while the French pursued some other objective than a pitched battle. This preference for firing on the

Redoutable, without a stick standing, continues to exchange fire. (Art Archive)

68-POUNDER CARRONADE

The carronade fired a hollow spherical shot from a bore whose careful crafting reduced windage – the narrow space between the bore and ball which enabled air to escape, so reducing a shot's velocity – thus conserving more power to drive a very large ball over a short range, making apt the weapon's sobriquet, 'the smasher'.

1. Sight
2. Vent
3. Elevating screw
4 Chock
5. Eyes for traversing tackle

6. Trucks (transverse wheels)
7. Breeching ring
8. Sliding bed
9. Eye for outhaul tackle
10. Carriage

11. Deck block
12. Pivot pin
13. Trunnion and bearing

VARIOUS FORMS OF AMMUNITION

1. Round shot
2. Bar shot
3. Chain shot
4. Knife or expanding shot (closed)
5. Grape shot
6. Canister shot
7. Cutaway view of a cartridge carrier
8. Knife shot (open)

Carronades in action. When loaded with round shot and fired at close range, this remarkable innovation in naval ordnance offered a tremendous smashing power that ordinary 'great' or 'long' guns could not match. Only the British had carronades at Trafalgar. (Angus Konstam)

rigging is revealed by the differing amounts of disabling ammunition carried by the French compared to the British. Whereas the French supplied each gun with ten rounds of double-headed shot, bar shot, chain shot and other, similar forms of ammunition, the British supplied only three rounds to each. The French also provided ten rounds of grape or canister to each gun, as compared with between three and seven for the British. Moreover, unlike the British, prior to battle the French hung grape and bar shot on hooks attached to the ship's side.

GUNNERY EQUIPMENT

Each gun was accompanied by a host of equipment necessary to move and fire it:

1 stool bed – Loosely fitted on the carriage to support the gun breech and the quoin.

1 quoin (sometimes two) – Wedge-shaped block placed on the stool bed in order to adjust the elevation.

1 rammer on a stave – Used to ram the gunpowder cartridge, shot and wads down the muzzle.

1 sponge on a stave – Used to sponge out the gun to extinguish any smouldering debris that remained after discharge.

1 wadhook – Used to remove debris and any remains of an unburnt cartridge, as well as to unload the gun if it misfired.

1 pair of handspikes – One set was shared between two guns. These were stout pieces of wood used as levers to raise the gun breech to adjust the gun's elevation or depression, and for moving the carriage to the side or in any other direction.

1 flexible rammer and sponge – Used to load and sponge out the gun when circumstances would not permit the use of an ordinary rammer and sponge, such as when the port was closed or blocked by direct contact with an enemy vessel – and hence there being no space with which to extend the stave out of the port.

1 gunlock – Flintlock mechanism used to fire the gun in conjunction with a cord known as a lanyard.

1 length of slowmatch – If the gun was not fitted with a gunlock, or if the gunlock failed, the gun captain used a piece of rope which, having been soaked in saltpetre, burned continuously and was applied to the touch hole to effect ignition.

1 matchtub – Shortened barrel, filled with sand to prevent fire, which held several slowmatches.

1 salt box – Available for every two guns and contained two cartridges ready for immediate use.

1 powder horn – Filled with fine black powder used for priming the gun and gunlock; the gun captain or his second wore this on a cord slung diagonally over his back and shoulder.

1 sand scuttle – Used to extinguish fires and for sprinkling sand on to the deck to provide better traction for the men.

1 cartridge pricker – Thin rod of iron fashioned into a ring at one end, sharpened at the other, and used to pierce the cartridge when the gun was loaded, exposing the gunpowder to ignition.

1 vent reamer – Used to clear the vent/touch hole of carbon deposits that became encrusted after prolonged firing.

1 lead apron – As guns not in use were always left charged and ready to fire, a lead apron was fitted and tied over the vent of the gun to prevent accidental firing and to protect the firing mechanism or touch hole from corrosion.

French gun crew. While their equipment and weaponry were much the same as those of their British counterparts, French gunners could neither fire as accurately nor as rapidly. (Terry Crowdy)

Each gun was commanded by a 'gun captain', with varying numbers of men comprising the crew, depending on the size of the weapon. Navies seldom fixed these numbers officially, and in any event changing circumstances in combat soon altered the complement of a gun crew: some fell wounded or were killed; others were called away for other duties. That said, approximately seven men served a 32-pounder and six an 18-pounder. Crews grew larger – in theory doubled – if the ship was only engaged on one side, since those men from the unengaged side would move across the gun deck to assist their comrades, so enhancing efficiency and rate of fire. British crews were trained to fire

33

on the downward roll of the ship, with the intention of hitting the enemy's hull. This tended to inflict heavier casualties on enemy personnel and, if a shot happened to fall short, it might at least ricochet off the water and inflict some damage. Shots fired against the rigging could of course inflict considerable, even crippling damage, but they might also pass harmlessly over the decks with minimal adverse effect.

Irrespective of the target, guns were aimed in the same manner in all three fleets present at Trafalgar. A gun's elevation could be changed by employing a wooden wedge known as a quoin, which, when inserted under the breech of the barrel, could elevate

VICE-ADMIRAL PIERRE DE VILLENEUVE

Pierre Charles Jean Baptiste Sylvestre de Villeneuve, commander of the Combined Fleet at Trafalgar, was born in 1763, making him only 42 at the battle. Descended from a distinguished aristocratic family that could trace its warrior traditions back to the Crusades, Villeneuve entered the French navy in 1778 and served under Admiral de Grasse in the West Indies, where he was present at the capture of Tobago. In 1793, he was promoted to *capitaine de vaisseau* (captain of a ship of the line) and met the young Napoleon Bonaparte, then a mere captain in the army, at the siege of Toulon. Villeneuve's aristocratic roots led to his suspension from command by the revolutionary government, but in 1795, as a result of the dearth of competent naval officers, he was restored to command and appointed naval chief of staff at Toulon.

Villeneuve was made *contre amiral* (rear-admiral) in 1796 and two years later commanded the right wing of the French fleet under Admiral Brueys at the battle of the Nile, from which, despite the destruction of virtually the whole of the French Mediterranean fleet, Villeneuve managed to escape with two ships of the line and two frigates. In May 1804, with the proclamation of the Empire, he was promoted to vice-admiral and appointed to command the fleet at Toulon in December. In March 1805, he left Toulon and made for the West Indies, pursued by Nelson, before returning to European waters and unexpectedly encountering Sir Robert Calder's squadron off Cape Finisterre, fighting an indecisive action which foiled his master's plan to combine the various French squadrons in the Channel as the vital prerequisite for

an invasion of England.

Villeneuve fought bravely at Trafalgar, though he was forced to strike his colours and was captured. Sent to Britain, he lived on parole in Hampshire for several months, during which time he watched Nelson's funeral procession in London. In April 1806 he was exchanged and returned to France where he committed suicide, probably as a result of the naval minister's failure to reply to his letter requesting a court martial by which Villeneuve hoped to exonerate himself. In his suicide note he bade farewell to his family and praised several deserving captains, but he died without having learned the reason behind Dumanoir's failure to assist the centre and rear of the Combined Fleet at Trafalgar. (Author's collection) it as much as +10 degrees or depress it to -5 degrees. The carriage itself could be aimed – or in correct parlance, pointed – in the direction of the target, though not with any great precision, by adjusting the gun tackle and, more crudely with additional muscle power, by manhandling the carriage with handspikes or crowbars.

Maximum range for the heavier guns situated on the lower decks was approximately 2,000 yards, though effective range was much shorter; hence the preference for some ship captains, particularly the British, to close with the enemy so that gunners could fire at point-blank range – 600 yards for their 32-pounders – or, if possible, to within 200 yards so their 24-pounders could fire in like manner. Thus, if in looking down the barrel of a gun at 100 yards the gun captain had a clear line of sight to his target, there was no need to adjust the elevation of the gun to account for gravity. That is to say, where the distance was sufficiently short that the shot would hit the target before the force of gravity altered its course in a downward trajectory, the target may be said to be at 'point-blank' range. Contemporaries often referred to such a distance as falling within 'pistol shot'.

Contrary to popular belief, ships did not issue successive broadsides, whereby all the guns on one side of the ship fired simultaneously, with the occasional exception of the opening salvo. Sustained firing of this kind would have produced undue shock to the structure of the ship and to the nerves of the crew; hence, in response to the order, 'fire as you bear', guns were discharged at the discretion of the individual gun captains as the target came both into view and range, producing something of a ripple effect down the length of the ship. Thereafter, guns were fired as rapidly as they could be re-loaded and 'run out' (rolled forward so the muzzle protruded through the port).

Redoutable takes on *Victory* and *Téméraire* simultaneously. (Art Archive)

GUNPOWDER

By the time of Trafalgar, gunnery had changed comparatively little in the previous two centuries, whether on land or at sea, and scant attention had been paid to experimentation, such that gunnery was at least as much an art as a science. British naval gunnery in 1805 rested largely on the results of work conducted 30 years before by a Dr Hutton, who, in drawing up a table to facilitate accurate firing, studied such factors as the velocity of the ball, the amount of powder required to throw that object a given distance, the length of the gun's bore, the effect of gravity on the ball, its weight and its point of impact – all with the aid of algebraic formulae based on the principles underlying Newtonian physics. Having perfected these calculations, Hutton determined the correct weight of powder required to propel a given weight of shot the distance desired.

Gunpowder therefore had to be manufactured to a consistent standard with respect to the relative proportion of its constituents – nitre (i.e. saltpetre), sulphur and charcoal. These were mixed in a granulated form, so proportioned as not merely to be combustible but capable of releasing sufficient force to carry a ball a great distance at high speed. The different proportions of these three vital ingredients need not be exactly the same in order to achieve the desired effect and each of the three navies at Trafalgar produced gunpowder to slightly different proportional specifications, thus:

	Britain	France
Saltpetre	75lb	75lb
Sulphur	10lb	9 ½lb
Charcoal	15lb	15 ½lb

According to *Falconer's New Universal Dictionary of the Marine*, a guide for mariners of this period:

> To make gunpowder ... regard is to be had to the purity or goodness of the ingredients, as well as the proportions of them, for the strength of the powder depends much on that circumstance, and also on the due working or mixing of them together. These three ingredients, in their purest state, being procured, they are then mixed together, in the proportion of six parts nitre, one part sulphur, and one part charcoal; the latter containing one-third in weight more than the sulphur.

Success lay in the mixture as well as in the measurement, for after being reduced to a fine dust, the chemicals had to be moistened with water, vinegar, urine or wine spirit, then crushed together with a mortar and pestle into a paste that in turn was dried and converted into grains, a process known as corning. The finest quality powder was reserved for use in pistols and muskets; a much cruder version sufficed for naval guns. Barrels of gunpowder were safely stored deep in the hold of the ship, and of course in the form of cartridges held in the magazine, known to contemporaries as the 'powder room'.

SMALL ARMS

Apart from its complement of heavy ordnance, a ship carried an array of hand-held weapons meant for use in close action. Small arms came in two types: pistols and muskets, the latter consisting of the 'sea service' model issued by the respective nation's board of ordnance, with a shorter barrel (about 39in.) – owing to the narrow confines of the ship – than the land pattern carried by infantry. Muskets were used during raids ashore or to fire volleys at close quarters against enemy sailors and marines on the decks of opposing vessels. They could be fitted with bayonets when boarding, though seamen usually preferred to wield them as clubs once fired, for there was no time to reload them in the heat of battle. At all but the closest distances – perhaps under 50 yards – this smoothbore weapon was hopelessly inaccurate except in the hands of a veteran shot. As one soldier of this period observed, a musket ball:

> will strike a figure of a man at 80 yards; it may even ... at 100, but a soldier must be very unfortunate indeed who shall be wounded by a common musket at 150 yards provided his antagonist aims at him; and as to firing at a man at 200 yards with a common musket, you may as well fire at the moon and have the same hope of hitting your object. I do maintain and will prove whenever called upon that no man was ever killed at 200 yards by a common musket by the person who aimed at him.

This conclusion, applied to fighting on land, was widely shared by contemporaries; one can only imagine how much more problematic were conditions at sea, with both ships rolling with the swell and shuddering violently under the constant, yet irregular discharge of the guns. One soon appreciates why captains instructed

French sailor. Though inexperienced and ill-trained, the French fought with considerable spirit, especially in ship-to-ship actions. (Umhey Collection)

OVERLEAF
British officers, ratings and marines from the *Tonnant* board and capture the *Algésiras*. *Tonnant*'s first broadside had brought down the French 74's mizzenmast, after which, in the course of close manoeuvring, the two ships became locked together in a deadly embrace. Using carronades, the *Tonnant* repelled a French attempt to board, and after a further hour of fire exchanged over the decks, the British captured their opponent in the manner shown. After hauling down her colours, the gallant ship counted losses of 219 killed and wounded, including both Admiral Magon and Captain Le Tourneur mortally so.

sailors and marines to withhold small-arms fire until the enemy was very close at hand indeed.

Pistols were even less accurate and thus were employed only during boarding, or when repelling boarders. These weapons were often carried in pairs and suspended from a brace, since the speed and chaos of hand-to-hand fighting rendered virtually impossible the opportunity to reload. In instances where a boarder carried only one pistol, he necessarily wielded an edged weapon in his other hand or carried it tucked into his belt. An officer of the period wrote:

> According to the custom prevailing from the earliest period of naval history to the present day, in boarding or opposing boarders, the pistol is held in the right hand, and in the attempt to board is fired and thrown away to enable the boarder to draw his cutlass, which yet remains in the scabbard or left hand.

Other proponents, including one unnamed officer, suggested using the pistol only as a last resort, at within three or four yards' range: 'A man armed with a pistol ought to reserve his fire to the last extremity if his life is to depend on the discharge of his pistol killing the man opposed to him.' That action having placed the weapon temporarily out of a commission in its capacity as a firearm, the heavy, brass-plated butt end could be wielded as a makeshift club.

EDGED WEAPONS

For centuries the cutlass was the standard, traditional weapon of the sailor. Its simple, unadorned hilt, which could act as a knuckle-duster when opponents confronted one another at extremely close quarters, supported a heavier blade than a sword. At the time of Trafalgar, the Royal Navy had yet to develop a standard system of drill for the use of the cutlass, though some officers devised their own instructions for guarding, thrusting and parrying. The straight edge of the cutlass was deadly enough, though an ill-directed blow did not necessarily put an adversary *hors de combat*, which explains some officers' recommendation that their men employ the point in the style of heavy cavalry, who were trained to thrust the blade into the adversary rather than slash at him as practised by the light cavalry, who wielded a lighter, curved blade. In handling a cutlass, one naval officer advised:

> Eagerness and heat in action, especially in a first onslaught, ought never to be the cause of a man putting himself so much off his guard … as to lift his arm to make a blow with his cutlass… But on the contrary, by rushing sword in hand straight out and thereby the guard maintained, and watching his opportunity of making the thrust, the slightest touch of the point is death to his enemy.

Known to contemporaries as a 'tomahawk', the boarding axe had a curved blade for hacking at the enemy or cutting away fallen rigging, and a sharpened point opposite the blade, which could be driven into the side of an enemy ship as an improvised foothold during boarding. Officers invariably carried slightly curved, often ornately decorated, swords, while the dirk, a compromise between a short sword and a dagger, was the characteristic weapon of midshipmen. Many seamen used pikes in close combat, either the full-length 8ft shaft of hardened ash tipped with a triangular-shaped steel blade, or the half-length version for fighting in more confined areas of a ship. Pikes were often stowed upright around the masts for easy accessibility. Swords and pistols were usually kept in barrels on the gun decks, though officers preferred to carry their own: unaccountably, as it happened, Nelson did not affix his sword and scabbard to his belt on the morning of Trafalgar.

Approaching battle at Trafalgar, about noon on 21 October 1805. Nelson's tactic of cutting the enemy's line was neither new nor unique to him, but his version, employing two parallel columns, with *Victory* leading the weather, and *Royal Sovereign* the lee column, was unique and daring.

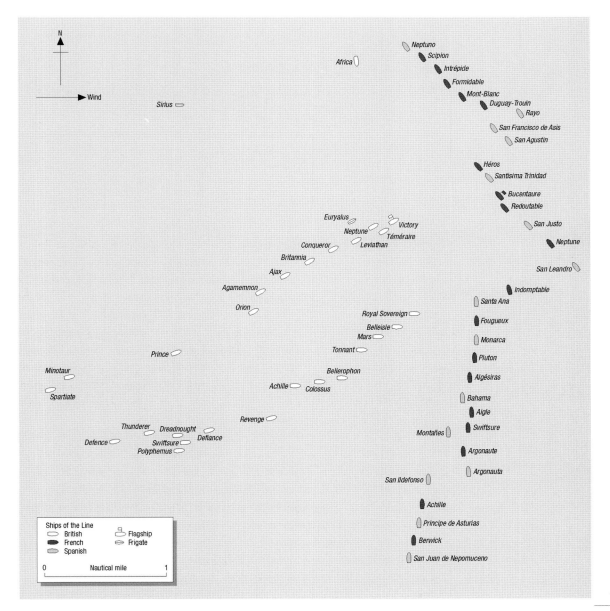

STRATEGIC SITUATION

THE RIVAL FLEETS

The Royal Navy was exceptionally large in 1805; indeed it was the largest navy in the world, with 181 ships of the line on the books, supported by 188 frigates. Yet the fighting force available to Nelson in the autumn of that year was only 27 ships of the line. In short, the 'paper' strength of the navy was never an accurate reflection of 'effective' or 'operational' numbers; for instance, 26 of the 181 ships of the line were under construction or had been ordered by the Admiralty. Thirty-nine vessels were deemed fit only for harbour service, whilst another 33 required extensive repairs, known as a refit, and were thus laid up in port. Once these numbers are deducted, only 83 first, second and third rate ships were available for service at sea, of which Nelson commanded about a third in his capacity as commander-in-chief of the Mediterranean Fleet. Even from this figure of 83 must be deducted those vessels that were worn out from constant service, for years of patrolling, escorting merchant vessels and blockade duty had taken a heavy toll on ships whose average age in 1805 was 17 years. Moreover, those still at sea and in great need of repair were not considered fit to take on the Franco-Spanish fleet, whenever it might materialize.

Fifty-six British ships of the line were, therefore, ready for action, but again this number must be viewed in context, for Britain's naval commitments extended across the globe, with responsibilities in the Irish Sea, the North Sea and, above all, the Channel, which naturally required the highest concentration of British naval power.

In addition there was escort duty for merchant vessels, protecting the coast of Canada and patrolling such distant theatres of operation as the South Atlantic, the West Indies and the Indian Ocean. Even within the all-important Channel Fleet, some ships were not available for immediate service in battle, for they were required to observe the French ships bottled up in Brest, Cherbourg, Lorient, Rochefort and elsewhere. All these factors account for the modest size of Nelson's command during the autumn of 1805.

Against this force the French had 41 ships of 54 guns or greater in commission, though of these only 33 mounted 74 guns or more – and were thus considered large enough to bear up to the sort of punishment that even the most heavily armed adversaries – the first and second rates – could inflict in the course of a day's engagement. To serve these ships the French had 14,400 personnel in their *Corps Impérial de l'Artillerie de la Marine*. Nonetheless, by the time of Trafalgar the navy was chronically short of manpower at sea, quite apart from its inability to maintain dockyard facilities, coastal installations and forts in a reasonable state of activity and defence. Both Brest and Toulon required hundreds of additional carpenters and massive supplies of oak for the construction of more vessels. In spite of all these deficiencies, in March 1805, Admiral Pierre de Villeneuve, the commander-in-chief of the Combined Fleet, finally put to sea with a respectably sized force. The French had not as yet assembled a truly formidable fleet, for their ships were widely dispersed, with many still bottled up by blockading British squadrons. Specifically, 21 ships of the line stood at anchor in Brest, 11 were at Toulon, and nine more were divided between Rochefort, Ferrol, and Cadiz, giving a total of only 41, as compared with 56 available to the British – though only 27 of which, as discussed above, would actually comprise Nelson's force at Trafalgar. Even if all these individual French squadrons could break free into the open sea, they had still to rendezvous in order to put their strength to best use – no

Toulon, the principal French naval base in the Mediterranean. Consisting of an inner harbour capable of holding 30 ships of the line and an equal number of frigates, Toulon boasted a superb dock, arsenal and victualling yard, plus an outer harbour and roadstead with space for three or four line of battle ships. Hills surrounded the harbour, which was protected by fortified batteries and four coastal forts. (Author's collection)

Cadiz, on the south-western coast of Spain, from which Villeneuve and the Combined Fleet emerged just prior to the battle of Trafalgar. Cadiz was one of Europe's best natural harbours, with impressive fortifications and dockyard facilities and ample space as a fleet anchorage. (Author's collection)

mean feat in an age of primitive communications. Until that time, Villeneuve would command a numerically – not to mention qualitatively – inferior force. Partial compensation for this deficiency was to be found by exploiting the naval power of her new ally, the third greatest maritime nation: Spain.

The Spanish fleet was divided into three parts, each section docked at its home port: Cadiz, Ferrol and Cartagena, though there were minor bases such as at Guarnizo (near Santander) and overseas stations such as at Havana, where more 74s were built in the 18th century than in any home port. All Spanish shipyards were government run, unlike in Britain, where private yards were used together with the Royal dockyards. The navy conscripted sailors according to the number desired from each province, but officials consistently failed to meet their quotas. Gunners were supplied from the 20 brigades of naval artillery, but while their numbers approximated their counterparts in British service, the majority were in fact conscripted landsmen. Of those who were actually sailors, only a small number had much in the way of experience in the open sea as opposed to coastal duties. The problems of manning the fleet were compounded by a yellow fever epidemic that struck southern Spain – precisely the area that served and supplied Cadiz – in the months and years immediately prior to Trafalgar. In February 1805 alone, a quarter of the inhabitants of Malaga succumbed to the disease. Failure to stem the tide of disease on land in an age of ignorance may be forgiven; but the neglect by naval authorities to issue lemon juice to Spanish crews to combat scurvy – despite all the evidence as to its efficacy – is not. Finally, while ships of the line often boasted a full complement of men, the numbers alone were deceptive, for the navy crowded its ships with soldiers in a counter-productive attempt to compensate for the severe shortage of trained sailors. Thus, aboard some Spanish vessels at Trafalgar, only 20 per cent of the crew could be classified as trained seamen. Nor was the number of commissioned ships of the line especially great: in 1805 Spain possessed 29 vessels of 74 guns or more, with an average age of 24 years. Of these, only 15 ships of the line would fight at Trafalgar.

FRENCH PLANS

The state of uncertainty at sea that had remained in place since the start of the war in May 1803 finally came to an end in March 1805 when, his earlier invasion plans of 1804 having gone awry, Napoleon issued orders to his commander-in-chief, Admiral Villeneuve, to evade the British blockade of Toulon, the great French port on the Mediterranean, make for Cadiz and release Admiral Don Federico Gravina's Spanish ships. Then he was to proceed to the West Indies to rendezvous with other squadrons released from their confinement at Brest, Ferrol and elsewhere, before returning to European waters to exploit their unassailable advantage in numbers. Still, brilliant though Napoleon was as a strategist and tactician on land, he had a poor understanding of the realities of naval warfare, and his plan failed to account for the huge distances involved in combining the various French and Spanish squadrons into a single, overwhelming force; nor was he capable of appreciating the vicissitudes of wind, weather and ocean current, not to mention the delays and potential losses imposed by a chance encounter with the enemy.

Napoleon's complex plan ran as follows: Admiral Villeneuve at Toulon with 11 ships of the line and six frigates was to run past the British blockading fleet under Vice-Admiral Lord Nelson, sail to Cadiz on the southern coast of Spain, drive off the small force of British ships observing that port, summon the Spanish ships to join him, and then make for Martinique in the West Indies. Meanwhile, Admiral Missiessy, who had previously left Rochefort, was to avoid battle with the British and proceed to Martinique to rendezvous with Villeneuve. The French squadron at Brest was to escape and then release the Spanish ships bottled up in Ferrol before also sailing to the West Indies. If all went as intended, the combined force assembled in the Caribbean could number as many as 80 ships of the line and 12 frigates – an irresistible number which, after reaching Ushant off the Breton coast, would almost certainly reach the Channel unmolested. All squadrons were to avoid contact with any large British force so that the Combined (Franco-Spanish) Fleet could reach its ultimate destination ready to fight and to escort the invasion force.

Napoleon's plans unravelled almost from the start. Admiral Honoré Joseph Antoine Ganteaume, with a fleet of 21 ships of the line at Brest, proved unable to break the blockade imposed by 15 British ships, for his orders specifically barred him from engaging the enemy in order to effect his escape. Each time Admiral Sir William Cornwallis's blockading squadron appeared to confront him, Ganteaume felt obliged to return to port, where he remained for the entire campaign. This also meant that for the moment the ships awaiting Ganteaume's arrival at Ferrol, on the northern coast of Spain, remained idle as well.

Nelson explaining his plan of attack to his captains just prior to Trafalgar. In an age of primitive communication, all commanders relied heavily on the fitness of their subordinates to act with their own discretion once battle commenced, for signals could not always be seen in the midst of battle. (Royal Naval Museum)

Admiral Missiessy reached the West Indies undetected, but when, by May, he found that Villeneuve was still not there, he returned to Rochefort. Villeneuve, meanwhile, left Toulon on 30 March and, owing to storms that blew Nelson off his station, managed to reach Cadiz and link up with Gravina. The two proceeded to Martinique, where, finding no other French squadrons present – Missiessy was almost back at Rochefort by this time – Villeneuve was told to proceed to Ferrol, release the blockaded ships there and then carry on to Brest to assist Ganteaume.

The British, for their part, carried on as before with the strategy developed by Lord Barham at the Admiralty. The Channel Fleet continued its watch on Brest, while Nelson pursued Villeneuve across the Atlantic in a bid to prevent the Combined Fleet from appearing in the Channel.

In June, aware that Nelson was in the West Indies, Villeneuve sailed east towards Ferrol, a journey, that owing to poor weather, took almost a month, and was blighted by the deaths of hundreds of his sailors from disease. On approaching his destination, many of his ships in a damaged state and large numbers of his men ill, Villeneuve encountered a British squadron under Sir Robert Calder on 22 July. Although inconclusive, the resulting battle off Cape Ortegal proved significant on a strategic level, for it convinced Villeneuve (who lost four ships in the engagement) to withdraw to Vigo on the north-west coast of Spain, with a consequent delay in the schedule to reach Brest. In mid-August Villeneuve, his ships now repaired, proceeded to Ferrol, released the ships there and thus increased his fleet to 30 ships of the line – an impressive force even if he was unsure as to its use.

Villeneuve was supposed to assist Ganteaume. However, to proceed north to Brest now seemed ill-advised, for he reasoned the British would by this time be aware of his intentions and would almost certainly have concentrated a large fleet at the mouth of the Channel, thus foiling the plan of invasion. Heading north with only 30 ships would bring on the very action that Napoleon had advised against; Villeneuve therefore turned south, reaching Cadiz on 22 August, four days after the weary Nelson, who had been unable to locate Villeneuve, reached Portsmouth to receive new orders. On 26 August, Napoleon's camp at Boulogne broke up and the crack 'Army of England' of over 100,000 men began an unanticipated but rapid march to the Danube, determined to destroy the forces of Austria and Russia then gathering to attack France. (Austria and Russia had concluded an alliance with Britain in April and August, respectively.) For Britain the immediate threat of invasion had passed, though the campaign at sea had yet to be played out. On 28 September, Villeneuve, still at Cadiz, received instructions to proceed into the Mediterranean and disembark troops in Naples before retiring to Toulon. Herein lay Nelson's chance finally to confront him.

With Villeneuve's location – though not his destination – now known, Nelson left Portsmouth in early September and proceeded south, reaching Admiral Cuthbert Collingwood, already on station off Cadiz, in mid-October, thereby increasing British strength to 27 ships of the line, against the 33 under Villeneuve. On the 19th, the first ships of the Combined Fleet began to emerge from port, the last reaching the open sea the following day after delays caused by light winds. By late afternoon on the 20th, Villeneuve was heading towards Gibraltar, only to reverse course on the following morning when he realized that Nelson's approach might leave him under strength if the Franco-Spanish van (the foremost element of the Combined Fleet) continued on course into the Mediterranean without the centre and rear in close support. Having changed tack, Villeneuve established a ragged, somewhat concave line, towards which Nelson and Collingwood, each commanding separate columns, approached with their respective flagships, the *Victory* and *Royal Sovereign*, leading the way. The battle was about to begin.

ADMIRAL DON FEDERICO GRAVINA

Born in Palermo in 1756 to an aristocratic family, Gravina joined the Spanish navy at the age of twelve in 1768. His first experience of operations took place between 1779 and 1782 at the siege of Gibraltar, where in the last year of operations he commanded a bomb vessel in the final, unsuccessful attack against the Rock. Gravina's boat was set alight by red-hot shot, an innovative use of ammunition by the British, and he was promoted to service aboard the massive *Santisima Trinidad*, the largest vessel afloat, fighting in the action off Cape Spartel against Lord Howe in 1782. In 1789, he was promoted to commodore and made one of the fastest journeys to South America in a frigate ever recorded. He visited England in 1793 and, having been shown around Portsmouth naval base, drew up a secret report about Royal Navy ships, gunnery and technology, with which he was duly impressed. In 1800 he served in Santo Domingo, a Spanish colony on the island of Hispaniola, and three years later became ambassador in Paris, where he befriended the French Minister of the Marine, Denis Decrès. He was present at Napoleon's coronation in 1804 and played a significant role in the negotiations that resulted in the Franco-Spanish alliance concluded in January 1805. On his promotion to commander-in-chief of the Spanish Navy, Gravina was sent to Cadiz to undertake preparations for joint service with Villeneuve.

In April 1805, on Villeneuve's arrival off Cadiz, Gravina joined him with six ships of the line and sailed for the West Indies and back, taking part in July in the action against Sir Robert Calder, whose squadron captured two of Gravina's ships. He attempted to resign but was dissuaded from doing so by Manuel de Godoy, one of the king's chief advisors. At Trafalgar, Gravina was second-in-

command, leading the squadron of observation (consisting of twelve ships of the line, two frigates and a brig), flying his flag in the *Principe de Asturias* (112) aboard which he was injured in the elbow. In hospital in Cadiz, Gravina survived in great pain for over four months before dying of gangrene, a fate that might have been averted had surgeons amputated his arm before it was too late. (Umhey Collection)

THE COMBATANTS

The officers and seamen of the rival navies at Trafalgar shared much in common, apart from their respective levels of training and experience, in which the British could claim superiority. The navies also had different systems of recruitment, for whereas in the Royal Navy crews consisted of a combination of volunteers and men pressed into service, the French and Spanish navies drafted men according to a quota system based on region. Since Britain had no tradition of conscription, either in the army or the navy, the Admiralty attracted recruits by a combination of bounties, appeals to the patriotic sentiments of young men, promises of adventure, an escape from poverty – especially with the prospect of earning prize money – or service as an alternative to prison. Even these inducements failed to meet the navy's insatiable demands, whereupon the authorities resorted to a form of legal kidnapping known as impressment. A man with a distinctive maritime air about him – his manner and dress – or simply those who appeared physically up to the onerous tasks required of a man serving for years at sea, became targets of a press gang, consisting of an officer and perhaps half a dozen burly sailors, who literally accosted their prey in the street and did their best to make off with him to the dockside.

Sailors of the rival navies at Trafalgar shared much in common in terms of appearance. As only officers and marines wore a uniform whose design adhered to official regulations, seamen were left to dress effectively as they pleased, and hence the variety of apparel renders elusive any accurate description of a 'typical' sailor of the period. Still, some standard features appeared in the lower ranks of all navies, including the practice of wearing one's hair in a queue – a single braid at the back of the head. Clothing generally consisted of loose-fitting trousers, often flaring from the knee down to facilitate climbing, crouching and bending; a simple linen shirt, plain, checked, or striped, with or without a collar, and sleeves often rolled up; black leather shoes –

though seamen often preferred to perform their tasks bare-footed; and a scarf or bandana worn around the head or neck to absorb sweat, or as a skullcap for protection against the sun.

Similarly, conditions aboard ship were effectively identical across all three navies. Captains, commodores and admirals had their own quarters, as sometimes did other senior officers, but the bulk of a ship's company worked and slept on the gun decks, with no more personal space than the confines of their hammocks and the immediate, cramped area around which they worked, perhaps as a gunner, carpenter or sailmaker. Duties were physically demanding and often dangerous – particularly work aloft – and periods of rest were short. A system of watches prevailed aboard all ships, with few men receiving more than four hours' continuous sleep before they were roused to perform their assigned functions. Food was generally adequate in terms of quantity, but monotonous and sometimes downright foul, consisting of hard biscuit, cheese, varying amounts of unimaginatively cooked vegetables and heavily salted meat and, of course, alcohol, ranging in the Royal Navy from 'grog' – spirits diluted with water – to wine and beer in the French and Spanish navies.

Whereas the various French and Spanish fleets and squadrons had, for most of the period prior to Trafalgar, remained bottled up in port as a result of the British blockade, British crews remained at sea for months at a time, whether performing the tedious task of observing an enemy port, providing convoy service to a merchant fleet, or cruising the waters of the Channel, West Indies, Mediterranean or other important theatre of operations in search of a rival force to engage. This unremitting service at sea, though exceptionally taxing both physically and psychologically, gave British crews a decided edge in terms of experience in seamanship and shiphandling, not to mention in gunnery, for the obvious reason that ships confined to port could not practise firing their guns. As such, whereas a British crew might attain a rate of fire of perhaps one shot every minute and a half, a French or Spanish crew was lucky to achieve half that level of proficiency.

Boarding party. Face-to-face encounters between the crews of opposing ships of the line were rare, being more a feature of fighting between frigates, brigs and sloops. A boarding action typically lasted only a few – albeit ghastly – minutes, during which both sides wielded a host of edged weapons and firearms including pikes, muskets, cutlasses, pistols, dirks and boarding axes. (Royal Naval Museum)

Leave was seldom granted in the British service, for some sailors, a sizeable proportion of whom consisted of pressed men, were liable to desert at the first opportunity, despite the grave consequences if they were caught. Punishments in all navies were severe, even in an age of brutish existence and execution for crimes that today are barely deemed worthy of imprisonment. Flogging constituted the standard punishment for a whole range of infractions from fighting, stealing, laziness and drunkenness, to more serious crimes like assaulting an officer, desertion or mutiny. Thus, a captain who ordered the boatswain's mate to inflict a dozen lashes on a reprobate was by no means considered harsh, for some offences could invite hundreds.

Illness and accident were commonplace aboard ships of this period, though seldom from scurvy – the source of that affliction, an acute shortage of Vitamin C, had been discovered and ameliorated by the late 18th century, apart from in the Spanish service. Yet there

HAND-HELD WEAPONRY

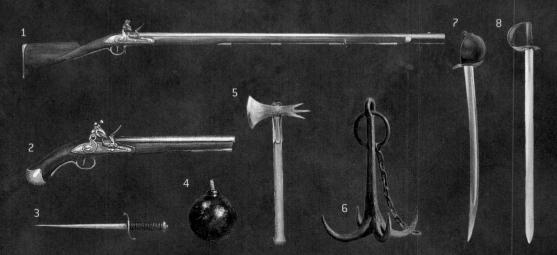

1. Smooth-bore sea-service flintlock musket; a slightly shorter model than its army counterpart, but still carries a bayonet
2. Pistol
3. The dirk was only carried by British sailors as a personal weapon and it was usually the preserve of midshipmen. The blade was longer than a dagger but shorter than a sword
4. Grenade; thrown from the rigging onto crowded enemy decks
5. Boarding axe; used either as a weapon or to cut away grapnels or ropes when ships were alongside one another
6. Grappling hook; smaller versions of these could be thrown by hand or the larger versions would hang from the yards to be dropped down onto smaller enemy ships
7. French cutlass with a distinctive curved blade and protected grip
8. British cutlass; noteworthy for its heavy, straight blade

Artwork by Steve Noon © Osprey Publishing

were a host of other scourges, including cholera, dysentery, yellow fever and more. As much of life aboard ship involved great physical exertion, including the lifting of heavy objects, raising anchors and adjusting massive sails, hernias ranked highest amongst the various injuries a sailor was likely to encounter in the course of his time at sea. Unfortunately, doctors' primitive understanding of medicine at this time yielded poor results, with death quite common for those suffering from fever, a serious injury or wound. In the case of the latter, the triage system had yet to be adopted, such that men were treated strictly in the order in which they appeared on the orlop deck, irrespective of the severity of their wounds. The not unsurprising result was that many men died of blood loss or shock before any of the various crude forms of treatment – which in the case of gunshot or fragment wounds to the extremities almost invariably meant amputation – could even be attempted.

COMBAT

French sailors perched in the fighting top of a ship of the line. Tops were large platforms mounted on the masts, from which men could work on the rigging or issue fire during battle. It was almost certainly a musket-armed French seaman in the mizzen top of the *Redoutable* who fired the shot that killed Nelson. (Terry Crowdy)

PREPARING FOR BATTLE

Battle was usually preceded by a period of manoeuvre, which could last for days. Both sides stalked one another, looking for a position of advantage, while the rival crews carried on with their usual routines. All this changed once one or both sides made a decision to engage. Sounding general quarters, a captain expected to have his ship ready for action within 30 minutes, with the speed and efficiency of his crew being a matter of personal pride. Meanwhile, if necessary, the admiral would signal the fleet to assume formation, usually 'line of battle' – that is, all vessels sailing single file, bow to stern of the vessel ahead.

On orders from the captain, the boatswain shouted, 'All hands!', upon which, aboard a British ship, a marine drummer boy began a drum roll, beating 'to quarters'. Aboard a French or Spanish vessel this sometimes came in the form of a sounding horn, either of which called the crew to battle stations (their appointed positions) and galvanized their sense of purpose. With great speed and agility,

51

topmen – those particularly fit and agile sailors responsible for working aloft – clambered into the rigging, sometimes over 100ft into the upper shrouds, to furl all those sails unnecessary for the ship's movement in battle, and so as to reduce the risk of fire. In the tops, marines armed with muskets and grenades took up their positions, and hauled up swivel guns or cohorns to mount by the topmast shrouds. Below, hundreds of other men raced to their posts to perform those tasks for which they had been drilled for months or even years. If time permitted, the captain would ensure that his crew was fed and issued with their rum ration, and the galley fire was extinguished. In the midst of these preparations, the officers usually changed into their best uniforms – cocked hat, gold-braided long coats, close-fitting white breeches, silk stockings and polished black leather shoes.

William Robinson, aboard the 74-gun *Revenge*, described the preparations being made throughout the British fleet on the morning of Trafalgar:

> During this time each ship was making the usual preparations, such as breaking away the [partitions of the] captain and officers' cabins, and sending all the lumber below – the doctors, parson, purser and loblolly men [surgeon's assistants], were also busy, getting the medicine chests and bandages out; and sails prepared for the wounded to be placed on, that they might be dressed in rotation, as they were taken down to the after cock-pit. In such a bustling, and it may be said, trying as well as serious time, it is curious to note the different dispositions of the British sailor. Some would be offering a guinea for a glass of grog, whilst others were making a sort of mutual verbal will, such as, if one of Johnny Crapeau's shots [a term given to the French] knocks my head off, you will take all my effects; and if you are killed, and I am not, why, I will have yours, and this is generally agreed to. During this momentous preparation, the human mind had ample time for meditation and conjecture, for it was evident that the fate of England rested on this battle…

On the forecastle (pronounced fo'c'sle), the forward-most deck on the ship, powder monkeys – young, fleet-footed boys – emerged from the hatches clutching powder cartridges for all the guns mounted along the upper decks, the same function taking place on the lower gun deck, as well. On the forecastle and along the ship's waist, sailors strained at block and tackle to lower longboats, which during the fighting could be used to carry messages to other ships in the line of battle. Meanwhile, the decks were strewn with sand to provide more traction for the usually barefooted seamen and to soak up water and blood.

Marine lieutenants meanwhile assembled their men amidships to prepare to snipe at the enemy from behind the makeshift barricade created by the tightly rolled hammocks stuffed into the netting that ran along the gunwales. A boatswain piped orders aloft for sailors to unfurl boarding nets to impede enemy sailors' attempts to mount a direct attack, while splinter nets were suspended above the upper decks to provide some protection from falling rigging. In the captain's cabin, sailors cleared the tackle off the guns, while carpenters removed the wooden bulkheads, partitions and furniture to make space for the gun crews at that station. As flying splinters caused the greatest number of casualties, everything that could impede the fighting efficiency of the ship or break up when struck by round shot was either placed aboard a ship's boat towed astern or carried below.

The ship's boat carried other, more unusual, cargo; men hurled livestock overboard while comrades in waiting boats plucked them out of the water and brought them aboard. There the animals would receive better protection from enemy fire and, more importantly, prevent them from creating a nuisance aboard ship once the firing began. Soon the boats were filled with chicken coops, goats and sheep, and officers' furniture, hauled up from the water by the boatswain's mates. The boats normally survived the battle intact, unless hit by random shot, but it was not uncommon for a ship to lose its entire supply of fresh meat in the course of the fighting. Objects that could not be stored aboard the ship's boats were stowed in the hold. By removing all the bulkheads and partitions the men created a series of continuous gun decks stretching the length of the ship, thus allowing the officers, midshipmen, marines and powder monkeys – that is, those members of a ship's company who had no fixed stations – to move about with as few hindrances as possible.

The captain (*capitain de vaisseau* and *capitan de navio* in the French and Spanish navies, respectively) positioned himself on the quarterdeck, together with the 1st lieutenant (*lieutenant en pied* in the French, and *teniente de navio* in the Spanish, service) and clerk, who took down information and orders. These in turn could be communicated to the topmen via a speaking trumpet. A midshipman (*aspirante* aboard a French, and *guardia marina* aboard a Spanish, ship) would be on hand serving as signal officer, bringing messages and conveying them to other parts of the ship. Several sailors would man the helm, behind which swung a row of fire buckets filled with water. Aboard the flagship, the admiral would continue to issue instructions to the fleet, the messages repeated by a series of frigates (hence the name 'repeating frigate' applied to this particular role) arrayed at intervals along the line of battle.

In the after cockpit the surgeon established his makeshift operating theatre, arranging his instruments, including saws and various blades. A tourniquet stood ready for use during amputation, while the operating table was prepared by covering the midshipmen's mess table with canvas or cloth. Anaesthetic, in the form of strong rum, was brought up from the spirit room, a bucket was placed close at hand to receive amputated limbs and a brazier heated to warm the surgical instruments to reduce the shock caused by contact with cold steel.

In the forward magazine, a gunner passed flannel-covered powder cartridges to an assistant who in turn passed them out to powder monkeys through safety screens fashioned from dampened blankets. Both men wore felt slippers to avoid producing sparks from static electricity. As the magazine by necessity had to be windowless, the men worked with the aid of a lantern situated behind a heavily paned glass compartment, an arrangement that provided light without risk of fire. Outside the magazine, as a powder monkey received a cartridge, he placed it inside a

Royal Marine. Marines served a variety of functions, including the maintenance of discipline aboard ship, preventing mutiny, guarding the captain and performing unskilled, laborious tasks such as bringing in the anchors or moving stores and equipment. In battle, marines issued musket fire against opposing crews, helped man the guns, fought in boarding parties and repelled those of the enemy. (Philip Haythornthwaite)

VICE-ADMIRAL HORATIO NELSON

The greatest sailor of his day and perhaps of any era, Nelson was born in 1758 to a Norfolk country pastor and joined the Royal Navy at the age of 12 through the patronage of his maternal uncle, Captain Maurice Suckling. Nelson was assigned to the *Raissonable* in 1771 and served in the West Indies for a year, later joining the *Triumph* and, in 1773, accompanying an expedition to the Arctic. Later that year he went to the East Indies but was invalided home in 1776 and transferred to the *Worcester* as acting lieutenant. He then returned to the West Indies, now a full lieutenant, aboard the frigate *Lowestoffe*.

Family connections enabled Nelson to obtain command of the brigantine *Badger* in 1778, with which he sought to protect British trade along the coast of Honduras from American privateers. He became a post captain in 1779 aboard the *Hinchinbroke* before serving at the beginning of the following year in the expedition against Fort San Juan, a remote Spanish position in Central America, where he nearly died of fever. Invalided home, on recovering he sailed in the *Albermarle* for Canada in 1782 and went on to the West Indies. While in command of the *Boreas* he tried to stop the illegal trade between American merchants and various British colonies.

On the outbreak of war in 1793 Nelson was given command of the *Agamemnon* (64) and joined Lord Hood's Mediterranean Fleet. He fought on Corsica, where he lost the sight of his right eye at Calvi in 1794, and was promoted to commodore in April 1796. In February 1797, at the battle of St. Vincent, Nelson distinguished himself by intercepting part of the fleeing Spanish fleet, taking two ships in rapid succession by boarding. Later that year, he led an unsuccessful attack against Tenerife, where his right arm was so severely wounded by grapeshot that it required amputation.

Appointed to command the *Vanguard* (74) in April 1798, Nelson rejoined the Mediterranean Fleet, his principal mission being to watch the Toulon fleet, whose destination was unknown. By the time he could make repairs following a severe gale, the French fleet had left port, but through persistence and an intensive search Nelson finally located it in Aboukir Bay, on the coast of Egypt, where he engaged Admiral Brueys and virtually

destroyed his force. Nelson returned home in 1800 and the following year served as second-in-command of the Baltic Fleet under Sir Hyde Parker, who sent Nelson to engage the Danes at anchor before Copenhagen, where they were defeated after a hard-fought action. Later the same year, Nelson led an abortive attack against the harbour at Boulogne in an attempt to disrupt French preparations for an invasion of England.

During the short peace between Britain and France in 1802–03, Nelson went ashore, only to return to sea upon the renewal of war in May 1803, this time in command of the Mediterranean Fleet. When Villeneuve finally left Toulon in the spring of 1805 Nelson pursued him to the West Indies and back, finally confronting the Combined Fleet at Trafalgar on 21 October, when in the course of shattering Napoleon's dream of the conquest of Britain, he fell mortally wounded. (Author's collection)

wooden, leather or metal 'salt box' before sprinting up the ladder to the gun to which he was assigned. At the base of the ladders a marine sentry stood to prevent anyone from fleeing below. In the hold the ship's pumps were readied, while carpenters prepared their supplies of oakum and other materials to plug holes created by enemy round shot. On the gun decks, men unlashed the guns from their secured positions, the gunner and his mates gathered shot and cartridges, and gun crews loaded their weapons with shot from the racks positioned around the ship's hatches.

The ship was now ready for action. Lieutenant Paul Nicholas described the look of the men aboard HMS *Belleisle* at this point:

> The determined and resolute countenance of the weather beaten sailor, here and there brightened by a smile of exultation was well suited to the terrific appearance which they exhibited. Some were stripped to the waist; some had bared their necks and arms; others had tied a handkerchief round their heads [to keep sweat from stinging their eyes]; and all seemed eagerly to await the order to engage.

As the ships closed, the bands aboard the British ships struck up such tunes as 'God Save the King', 'Rule Britannia' and 'Britons Strike Home'. The French conducted themselves somewhat differently; aboard the two-decked *Redoutable*, for instance, Captain Jean Lucas was pleased to see the colours run up with such *joie de vivre*: 'That of the *Redoutable* was done in an imposing manner: the drums were beating and the musketry presented arms to the standard; it was saluted by the officers and crew with seven cheers [of] '*Vive l'Empereur!*

Thus prepared, the opposing lines of battle met.

Nelson's famous signal at Trafalgar. Ever the consummate commander, the victor of the Nile and Copenhagen knew instinctively how to inspire his men, as his message testifies: 'England expects that every man will do his duty.' (Royal Naval Museum)

INTO ACTION

The British approached the Franco-Spanish line in two columns, one led by Nelson with 12 ships, and the other under Collingwood, with 15 ships. Lucas described the opening of the action thus:

> The enemy's column, which was directed against our centre, was at eleven o'clock on the port side, and the flagship *Bucentaure* began firing. I ordered a number of the captains of the guns to go up on the forecastle and observe why it was some of our ships fired so badly. They found all their shots carried too low and fell short. I then gave orders to aim for dismasting and above all to aim straight. At a quarter to twelve the *Redoutable* opened fire with a shot from the first gun division. It cut through the foretopsail yard of *Victory*, whereupon cheers and shouts resounded all over the ship. Our firing was well kept up, and in less than ten minutes the British flagship had lost her mizzenmast, foretopsail, and main topgallant mast.

Reference to the damage inflicted here is significant, for it revealed once again the French preference for firing at the rigging. Lieutenant Pierre-Guillaume Gicquel des Touches described the differences between the British and French methods in this respect:

Jean-Jacques Lucas, captain of the *Redoutable*, whose crew of 643 fought magnificently at Trafalgar and suffered 88 per cent casualties, including the severely wounded Lucas himself, who only surrendered when his ship had been reduced to a floating charnel house. (Royal Naval Museum)

The audacity with which Admiral Nelson had attacked us, and which so completely succeeded, arose from the complete scorn which, not without reason, he professed for the effects of our gunfire. At that time our principle was to aim at the masts and, in order to produce any real damage, we wasted masses of projectiles which, if they had been aimed at the hulls, would have felled a proportion of the crews. Thus our losses were always incomparably higher than those of the English, who fired horizontally and hit our wooden sides, letting fly splinters which were more murderous than the cannon ball itself.

Approaching as they did at roughly right angles to their enemy, the British could not return fire until they reached the Franco-Spanish line, which they proceeded to cut so as to engage the Combined Fleet from both port and starboard, in so doing creating a battle characterized by close-fought mêlées between pairs – but more often small groups of – ships, thus satisfying Nelson's final order: 'Engage the enemy more closely.'

This tactic suited British crews, whose superior rate of fire, issued whenever possible at short range, produced devastating effects. William Robinson witnessed first-hand the British preference for firing when close upon the enemy:

Typical British 'tar'. Noted for his coarseness, foul language and predilection for drink, 'Jack' possessed the redeeming virtue of being exceptionally skilful in the ways of the nautical world and formed the mainstay of the Royal Navy's success. (Philip Haythornthwaite)

> … many of our men thought it hard that the firing should be all on one side [i.e. being unable to return fire until their ships could be positioned athwart their opponents], and became impatient to return the compliment; but our captain had given orders not to fire until we got close in with them, so that all our shots might tell; indeed, these were his words: 'We shall want all our shot when we get close in; never mind their firing: when I fire a carronade from the quarter-deck, that will be a signal for you to begin, and I know you will do your duty as Englishmen.'

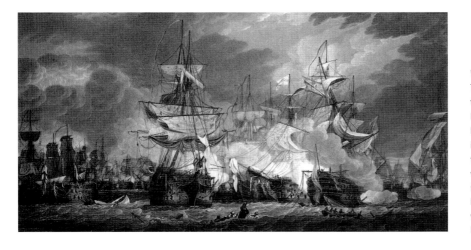

Victory cutting the line at Trafalgar. While Nelson's tactic of piercing the Franco-Spanish line threw his opponents into confusion, it carried inherent risks for the lead vessels, whose bows were exposed to concentrated fire during the approach, and had no opportunity with which to return fire. (National Maritime Museum)

FIRING THE GUNS

Firing sequence showing four critical phases in the handling of a long gun. For ease of view, the crew shown here is much reduced in numbers, which varied according to the size of the gun they fired. The *Victory*'s 32-pdrs had 14 men, the 24-pdrs had 11 and the 12-pdrs had nine. A French 36-pdr had a crew of 15, a 24-pdr had 13, an 18-pdr 11, a 12-pdr nine, an 8-pdr nine, and 6- and 4-pdrs five. These figures are for a pair of guns situated opposite one another. When a ship only needed to fire on one side, the entire gun crew served a single piece of ordnance.

The barrel is sponged out, a new cartridge, two wads and a round shot are rammed down the barrel. The gun captain inserts a priming wire into the vent (or touch hole), pricking the cartridge bag to enable a flame to communicate with the powder.

Having run the gun out of the port, the crew manhandles the weapon into position and adjusts the elevation of the barrel with a quoin. The gun captain then pours fine powder into the vent to prime the charge.

While the gun crew stands well back, the captain applies a slow match to the touch hole, igniting the priming powder and causing the gun to discharge.

The gun having fired and recoiled, the sequence is repeated, the sponge, round shot and cartridge being prepared.

Once both British columns pierced the Combined Fleet's centre – and in so doing isolated the van under Admiral Dumanoir from Villeneuve's centre and rear, both sides began to batter away at one another, sometimes while on parallel courses, sometimes in passing, often obliquely. Firing a gun was essentially the same in all three navies present at Trafalgar. After discharge the gun recoiled inboard to the farthest extent of its breeching rope, which prevented the weapon from rolling uncontrollably across the gun deck. The bore of the gun was then 'wormed' by a man wielding an implement with a twisted metal end which extracted any large debris, such as traces of unburnt cartridge from the previously discharged shot, so preventing the premature ignition of the next cartridge. An additional precaution, known as 'swabbing out', extinguished any smouldering material by following the procedure laid down in *Burney's Universal Dictionary of the Marine*:

> The sponge is to be rammed down [to] the bottom of the chamber, and then twisted round, to extinguish effectually any remains of fire; and when drawn out, to be struck against the outside of the muzzle, to shake off any sparks or scraps of the cartridge that may have come out with it and next its end is to be shifted ready for loading.

The 'end' referred to here was its opposite end, which consisted of a wooden rammer used to push the cartridge, wads and ammunition down the bore. A fresh cartridge, previously supplied by a powder monkey, was removed from the container into which it had been placed down in the magazine. Then, as Burney continues:

> The cartridge (with the bottom end first, seam downwards, and a wad after it) is to be put into the gun, and thrust a little way into the mouth, where the rammer is to be entered; the cartridge is then to be forcibly rammed down, and the [gun] captain, at the same time, is to keep his priming wire in the vent, and feeling the cartridge, is to give the word 'home' when the rammer is to be drawn, and not before.

A felt wad followed the cartridge, after which a gunner, having collected a round shot (or other desired form of ammunition) and a second wad from a rack to the rear of the gun rammed these home, thus sandwiching the shot between the two wads, the first of which – situated between the cartridge and the shot – was thought to aid ballistics, while the second wad prevented the shot from rolling out of the barrel as the ship swayed. Once reloaded, men wielded handspikes to sight the gun, employing them as levers beneath the carriage. Then, when preparing to 'run out' the gun, the crew planted their feet as firmly as possible and took up the slack on the side tackles. The weapon was then manoeuvred forward by pulling with all possible force on the tackles, which were attached to the carriage and braced to the side of the ship.

At the gun's breech, the gun captain jabbed the priming wire down the vent to pierce the flannel cartridge before priming the charge, by which he poured a small quantity of fine powder from his powder horn down the touch hole. To this was applied a lighted match, known as a linstock or slow match, which consisted of a piece of cord coiled around a length of slender wood. These were standard issue in

French and Spanish service at the time of Trafalgar, but had by this time been replaced in the Royal Navy by a much more reliable firing mechanism known as a gunlock. This device, mounted over the touchhole, looked very much like, and functioned almost identically to, the flintlock mechanism of a musket, the principal difference being the greater size and weight of the naval version. The use of a gunlock obviated the need to prime the charge with loose powder; instead, the gun captain inserted a goose quill filled with powder into the vent and cocked the gunlock. He then discharged the weapon by pulling on a lanyard which, owing to its length, enabled him to stand well clear of the gun so as to avoid the very unpleasant prospect of a gun wheel recoiling over his feet. On yanking the lanyard, the gunlock created a spark which was then transmitted down to the chamber via the goose quill, thereby causing ignition. The men held the tackle of the gun as it recoiled instantly upon discharge. If the mechanism misfired, a slow match could be retrieved from a sand-filled bucket nearby and applied to the touch hole. The gun having fired and recoiled, the sequence was repeated, with British gun crews achieving a rate of fire of perhaps one shot every ninety seconds, depending on conditions. No battle-tested statistics exist on rates of fire, but numerous eyewitnesses concur on the superior speed of British crews over all adversaries save the Americans.

Where ships confronted each other with their full broadsides to bear (as opposed to striking the enemy's stern, bow or quarter), round shot directed against the hull struck the ship where the timber was thickest – along its sides. If, however, an opponent was attacked from directly ahead or astern, known as raking or 'crossing the T', exceptionally severe damage was inflicted against the weaker bow or stern. Round shot crashing into these particularly vulnerable parts of a ship – so directed by gun captains firing in turn as their weapons came to bear – careened down the length of the enemy's deck, overturning guns and scattering men like ninepins.

The whole experience was hellish. Lieutenant Paul Nicholas, aboard the *Belleisle*, vividly described his ship's exchange with the *Fougueux*:

> My two brother officers and myself were stationed, with about thirty men [bearing] small arms, on the poop, on the front of which I was now standing. The shot began to pass over us and gave us an intimation of what we should in a few minutes undergo. An awful silence prevailed in the ship, only interrupted by the commanding voice of Captain Hargood, 'Steady! Starboard a little! steady so!' echoed by the master directing the quartermasters at the wheel. A shriek soon followed – a cry of agony was produced by the next shot – and the loss of the head of a poor recruit was the effect of the succeeding, and as we advanced, destruction rapidly increased... My eyes were horror struck at the bloody corpses around me, and my ears rang with the shrieks of the wounded and the moans of the dying.

The efficiency with which gun crews – and indeed all hands – could perform their functions was naturally inhibited by the noise, confusion and thick white smoke generated by the action. 'Often during the battle we could not see for the smoke,' Robinson recalled, '[or] whether we were firing at a foe or friend, and as to hearing,

ENGAGING THE ENEMY

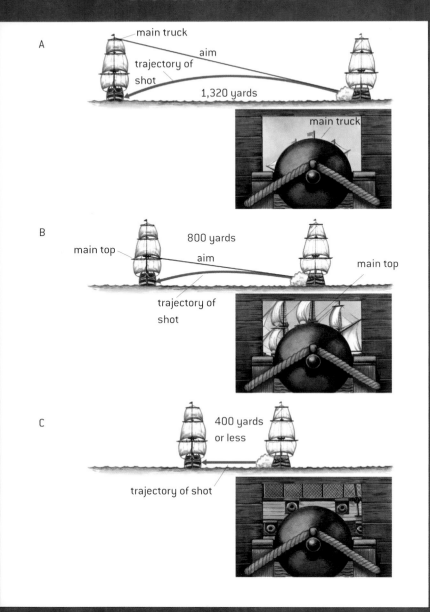

A — main truck / aim / trajectory of shot / 1,320 yards / main truck

B — 800 yards / main top / aim / main top / trajectory of shot

C — 400 yards or less / trajectory of shot

Aiming at extreme distance

When the distance to the enemy's hull measured approximately 1,320 yards on the waterline, the gunner aimed at the main truck of the opposing ship.

Aiming at moderate distance

When the distance to the enemy's hull measured approximately 880 yards on the waterline, the gunner aimed at the main top of the opposing ship.

Aiming at short distance

When the distance to the enemy's hull measured 400 yards or less, the gunner aimed directly at the hull of the opposing ship, since point blank range required no elevation of the gun. Broadsides delivered at less than 300 yards were particularly effective.

the noise of the guns had so completely made us deaf, that we were obliged to look only to the motions that were made.'

Smoke, noise and confusion were only the start, for as the fire intensified and the damage mounted, the crew found their ability to manage their vessel increasingly impaired. Robinson observed that, on being confronted by adversaries on both sides:

We were now unable to work the ship, our yards, sails, and masts being disabled, and the braces completely shot away. In this condition we lay by the side of the enemy, firing away, and now and then we received a good raking from them, passing under our stern. This was a busy time for us, for we had not only to endeavour to repair our damage, but to keep to our duty.

It may be instructive to pause here to relate the general course of the battle itself, details of which must, however, be left to more specialized studies (see Campaign 157: *Trafalgar 1805*). Nelson's plan, by which he and Collingwood were to drive through the Franco-Spanish centre with their respective columns, the former led by the *Victory* and the latter by the *Royal Sovereign*, have already been described. These ships naturally bore the brunt of the enemy's broadsides during the 40 minutes of approach under which they were within range. Nelson took the calculated risk that his opponents' slower and less accurate fire would fail to prevent the two columns from piercing the line; he was right, and both flagships issued devastating initial broadsides into the sterns of the ships, which they passed whilst breaking through the line. Villeneuve's flagship, the *Bucentaure*, is thought to have suffered as many as 200 casualties from the port guns of the *Victory* as Nelson passed astern.

The remaining British ships followed their next ahead, some confronting the French and Spanish centre and oncoming rear to windward, others to leeward. The battle now began in earnest, with individual ship's captains free to engage foes as they saw fit, with the British object to neutralize the Franco-Spanish centre before the rear could make its impact on the fighting properly felt and before the van could come about and reinforce the centre. Villeneuve lost no time in signalling Admiral Dumanoir, commander of the van, to reverse his northward course, but in failing to do so until after 1400hrs – whether Dumanoir failed to see the signal or refused to obey it is not clear – he left the centre and rear outnumbered and outfought, and even by 1530hrs Dumanoir's handful of ships had not yet reached the principal scene of action. In fact, by the time Dumanoir acted upon Villeneuve's signal, the Franco-Spanish centre had already broken up into a confused jumble of vessels, enabling the British to confront the rear in due course, confident of overpowering it as well.

Trafalgar. In piercing the Franco-Spanish line in two places, Nelson isolated the enemy van and initiated a mêlée at close quarters – precisely the sort of action in which superior British gunnery could be employed to its best advantage. Nelson did not conceive of this tactic, but rather employed it in brilliant fashion. (Art Archive)

One of the most heavily engaged ships at Trafalgar was the British 74, *Belleisle*, which by the end of the fighting would be reduced to a floating wreck – hardly surprising when considering that she had been set upon by multiple enemies firing 24lb shot capable of penetrating timber 2ft 6in. thick. Lieutenant Nicholas described some of the fearful damage his ship suffered at the hands of several assailants:

> At about one o'clock the *Fougueux* ran us on board the starboard side; and we continued thus engaging, until the latter dropped astern. Our mizzenmast soon went, and soon afterwards the maintopmast. A two-decked ship, the *Neptune*, 80 [actually with 84 guns], then took a position on our bow, and a 74, the *Achille*, on our quarter. At two o'clock the mainmast fell over the larboard [port] side; I was at the time under the break of the poop aiding in running out a carronade, when a cry of 'stand clear there! here it comes!' made me look up, and at that instant the mainmast fell over the bulwarks just above me. This ponderous mass made the ship's whole frame shake, and had it taken a central direction it would have gone through the poop and added many to our list of sufferers. At half-past two our foremast was shot away close to the deck.

But naval ammunition did more than simply damage ships: it caused the most appalling wounds. Even a single shot was capable of claiming several victims in rapid succession. Dr Beatty of the *Victory* noted that 'A double-headed shot struck one of the parties of Marines drawn upon the poop, and killed eight of them; [upon] his Lordship [Nelson], perceiving this, [he] ordered Captain Adair to disperse his men round the ship, that they might not suffer so much from being together.' Captain Servaux of the two-decker *Fougueux* described the effect of raking fire delivered against her bow by the *Royal Sovereign* as Collingwood broke the line around 1220hrs and:

> … gave us a broadside from five and fifty guns and carronades, hurtling forth a storm of cannonballs, big and small, and musket shot. I thought the *Fougueux* was shattered to pieces – pulverized. The storm of projectiles that hurled themselves against and through the hull on the port side made the ship heel to starboard. Most of the sails and rigging were cut to pieces, while the upper deck was swept clear of the greater number of the seamen working there, and of the soldier sharpshooters. Our gun-decks below, had, however, suffered less severely. There, not more than thirty men in all were put *hors de combat*.

Something of the confusion and jumble into which the battle dissolved once the 60 ships of the line had become intermingled is revealed from this Spanish account by Don Benito Pérez Galdós aboard the colossal *Santísima Trinidad*, then locked in deadly combat with Nelson's flagship:

> The [*Santísima*] *Trinidad* was doing the *Victory* immense damage, when the *Téméraire*, by a wonderfully clever manoeuvre, slipped in between the two vessels; thus sheltered by her consort from our fire. She then passed through the line astern of the *Trinidad*, and as the *Bucentaure*, during the firing, had moved up so close alongside the *Trinidad* that

their yardarms touched, there was a wide space beyond, into which the *Téméraire* settled herself, and then she came up on her lee side and delivered a broadside into us there. At the same time the *Neptune*, another large English ship, placed herself where the *Victory* had previously been, while the *Victory* also wore round, so that, in a few minutes, the *Trinidad* was quite surrounded by the enemy and riddled by shot from all sides.

The line of the Combined Fleet was after that broken in several points, and the loose order in which they had been formed at the outset gave place to disastrous confusion. We were surrounded by the enemy, whose guns kept up a tornado of round shot and grape-shot on our ship, and on the *Bucentaure* as well. The *San Agustín*, the *Héros*, and the [*San*] *Leandro*, were also engaged at some distance from us, where they had rather more sea-room, while the *Trinidad*, and the Admiral's ship, cut off on all sides and held fast by the genius of the great Nelson, were fighting desperately.

Once ships were fully engaged, gun decks resembled the infernal regions, with swirling smoke and belching fire. But while below decks the guns blazed away with a deafening roar, high above decks, in the tops, marines and seamen rained down fire from muskets, picking off easily recognizable officers and opposing topmen. At the same time, swivel guns, loaded with grapeshot, cut swathes through the enemy ranks on the decks below. To these the French, in particular aboard *Redoutable*, whose captain had specially trained his crew in their use, added grenades, whose fuses they lit with a slow match before hurling these orange-sized explosives down into the fray.

Those killed in battle were, as a matter of course, unceremoniously flung overboard, for their bodies could not be preserved for burial on land and, in any event, they posed immediate obstacles to those still engaged in the fighting. Robinson described this rather undignified procedure:

Orders were now given to fetch the dead bodies from the after cock-pit, and throw them over-board; these were the bodies of men who were taken down to the doctor during the battle, badly wounded, and who by the time the engagement was ended were dead.

The quarterdeck of the *Victory*, on which Nelson lies mortally wounded amidst the debris of battle. Once action commenced, ships' decks rapidly became strewn with severed lines, the dead and wounded, splintered timber, spent musket balls, fragments of naval ammunition and severed limbs. Blood was ubiquitous and flowed across the deck in rivulets with the roll of the ship. (Royal Naval Museum)

OVERLEAF
Crippled yet defiant: after over three hours' combat, fought mostly at close range against several enemy ships simultaneously, the mastless HMS *Belleisle* sits dead in the water, the guns of her starboard quarter masked by fallen rigging and sails. Undaunted, she continues to fight her French and Spanish adversaries as *Polyphemus*, *Defiance* and *Swiftsure* come to her relief.

On some occasions the mortally wounded shared this fate, while some more lightly wounded, yet unconscious and mistaken for dead, probably met their end in this way. Robinson recalled how a 32lb double-headed shot entered the lower deck port of the *Revenge*, killing and wounding nearly an entire gun crew, amongst them the ship's cobbler:

> He happened to be stationed at the gun where this messenger of death and destruction entered, and the poor fellow was so completely stunned by the head of another man being knocked against his, that no one doubted but that he was dead. As it is customary to throw overboard those, who, in an engagement are killed outright, the poor cobbler, amongst the rest, was taken to the port-hole to be committed to the deep, without any other ceremony than shoving him though the port: but, just as they were about to let him slip from their hands into the water, the blood began to circulate, and he commenced kicking. Upon this sign of returning life, his shipmates soon hauled the poor snob in again, and, though wonderful to relate, he recovered so speedily, that he actually fought the battle out...

A ship that suffered excessive structural damage and losses to its crew could – in recognition of the futility of further resistance and the inevitability of defeat – signal surrender by hauling down the national ensign, a gesture known as 'striking' or 'striking the colours'. This could be done with honour when it had become obvious that a crew had done all that could reasonably be expected by way of resistance and accounts for the widespread practice of ships flying several ensigns in battle: if one were shot away the others remained aloft to indicate that the vessel was still in action.

The badly wounded First Captain of the *Argonauta*, Don Antonio Pareja, found himself in just such a predicament:

> I handed over the command to the Second Captain. At this hour my ship had all the guns on the quarter-deck and poop dismounted, a great number of the guns in the batteries were out of action, as much on account of the result of the numerous dead and wounded

among them, according to the report of their officers. The whole rigging was utterly destroyed, so that there were no shrouds left to the masts – save one to the main-mast – and they were threatening to fall every minute, being shot through; in this situation it was very evident that this ship could make but slight and feeble resistance, having continually engaged with the same superior force ... my second ... inform[ed] me that over and above the injuries that we had already sustained, the ship was making much water from further ones [i.e. shot holes] that had occurred, and had lost her rudder, which fresh increase of damage in addition to the previous ones, held out no further prospect – the ship being disabled – save that of the sacrifice of those men who with the greatest spirit, courage and fearfulness of death, had rendered the greatest service and honour to the King's colours. Consequently, I replied to my second that – given the absolute impossibility of being able to do otherwise – he must act in accordance with the regulations, and at 3.30 in the afternoon he gave orders to haul down the colours ...

If, however, a ship refused to surrender, the issue could be decided by the attacker coming abreast of the stricken vessel, fastening the two together with grappling irons, and then boarding her, whereby a senior officer – sometimes the captain himself – led a body of men over the gunwales and onto the enemy's decks, where the issue was decided in grisly fashion a matter of minutes.

Having said this, boarding between ships of the line was a comparatively rare occurrence, this form of terrifying and bloody combat generally being carried on between frigates and smaller vessels. Nevertheless, crews were trained for this eventuality, with one or two men from each gun crew allocated to this service if required. The outcome was seldom certain; William Robinson described how boarders could be confounded in their scheme:

A Spanish three-decker ran her bowsprit over our poop, with a number of her crew on it, and, in her fore rigging, two or three hundred men were ready to follow; but they

The *Redoutable*, flying the Tricolore, fights the *Victory* to larboard and the *Téméraire* to starboard. Trafalgar was a critical engagement: not until Jutland in 1916 did Britain again fight a naval battle with so much depending on the outcome. (Art Archive)

caught a Tartar, for their design was discovered, and our marines with their small arms, and the carronades on the poop, loaded with canister shot, swept them off so fast, some into the water, and some on the decks, that they were glad to sheer off.

Boarding was also possible if the rigging of two vessels became entangled or, as contemporaries put it, 'fouled'. Captain Lucas of the *Redoutable*, on finding his ship's rigging hopelessly snarled with that of the *Victory*, sought to board by fastening the two ships together in more permanent fashion, a circumstance that made firing between the antagonists virtually impossible:

> In the end, the *Victory* not having succeeded in passing astern of the French Admiral [Villeneuve], ran foul of us, dropping alongside and shearing off aft in such a way that our poop lay alongside her quarter-deck. From this position the grappling irons were thrown on board her. Those at the stern parted, but those forward held on; and at the same time our broadside was discharged, resulting in a terrible slaughter. We continued to fire for some time, although there was some delay at the guns. We had to use rope rammers in several cases, and fire with the guns run in, being unable to bowse them, as the ports were masked by the sides of the *Victory*.

Lucas ordered most of his men on deck, from which they issued a tremendous hail of musket fire and threw hundreds of grenades on to the deck of the *Victory*. An odd situation then arose: most of the men on the upper decks of Nelson's flagship were now dead or wounded, including the admiral himself, almost certainly struck down by a musket ball fired from the mizzen top of the *Redoutable*, and yet below the guns of the *Victory* continued to smash the sides of her opponent, most of whose crew were on deck, preparing to board the nearly empty upper decks of Nelson's stricken vessel. Circumstances looked bleak for the *Victory*, but even as hundreds of cheering

Spanish sailors clinging to the wreckage of the *Santisima Trinidad*. Survival in the water very much depended on the presence of floating debris, for few sailors knew how to swim – a skill never encouraged by captains who perhaps feared it might facilitate desertion when dry land was accessible. (Philip Haythornthwaite)

Frenchmen were poised to board, the 98-gun *Téméraire*, a British three-decker, appeared through the haze and came alongside the *Redoutable*, sandwiching her between the two larger British ships. The guns of the *Téméraire* made havoc amongst the Frenchmen assembled on *Redoutable*'s upper decks, and Lucas was forced to abandon his plan. When this intrepid captain refused to surrender even as his ship was taking on water and large numbers of his crew lay wounded (including himself) and dying, the *Téméraire* took the *Redoutable* by boarding.

The fate of the *Redoutable* bears witness to the fact that warships were nothing if not stoutly built; indeed, sinking as a consequence of enemy fire was a very rare occurrence. Nor, in such cases, was the captain expected to go down with his ship – two myths concerning the age of sail that have unaccountably entered the popular mythology associated with this period. Unquestionably, ships were savagely riddled and pockmarked in battle, but even shot holes below the waterline could usually be stopped up by the carpenter and his mates before the vessel foundered, and all ships carried pumps that, though extremely laborious to operate, could clear the bilges once the more serious leaks were overcome.

More dramatic still than a sinking ship was its destruction as a result of explosion, as occurred to the French flagship *L'Orient* at the battle of the Nile in 1798 when flames reached her magazine. At Trafalgar, Lieutenant Cauchard described the growing crisis aboard the French 74, *Achille*, whose upper deck caught fire after the 98-gun *Prince* brought down her mainmast, leaving only the

HMS *Belleisle* standing defiantly at Trafalgar. Reduced to a floating wreck and completely dead in the water, this formidable vessel continued to offer resistance despite her desperate condition. (Author's collection)

foremast standing. Cauchard ordered the bilge cocks opened in order to flood the ship, together with other desperate measures:

> All hands then came on deck and, losing all hope of extinguishing the fire, we no longer attended to anything except saving the ship's company, by throwing overboard all the debris that might offer them the means of escaping from almost certain death and awaiting the aid that the neighbouring ships might send them.

As the flames spread, it became clear that the ship could not be saved and that a massive explosion was inevitable. The crew began to leap over the side and swim for the boats sent by the *Prince*, the cutter *Entreprenante* and the schooner *Pickle*. Those guns still loaded went off as the flames reached them and at about 1645hrs the ship disintegrated in a violent explosion, which Lieutenant Frederick Hoffman of the *Tonnant* described as 'sublime and awful'. An officer aboard the *Defence* also witnessed the catastrophe:

> It was a sight the most awful and grand that can be conceived. In a moment the hull burst into a cloud of smoke and fire. A column of vivid flame shot up to an enormous height in the atmosphere and terminated by expanding into an immense globe representing, for a few seconds, a prodigious tree in flames, speckled with many dark spots, which the pieces of timber and bodies of men occasioned while they were suspended in the clouds.

The destruction of the *Achille* marked the end of the action, as firing, almost in deference to the passing of that ship, began to fade away. Villeneuve's centre and rear had been shattered and he himself was a prisoner; Gravina, severely wounded, was fleeing northward with ten ships while Dumanoir with four was proceeding north-west under full sail for Cadiz.

Achille ablaze. By 1600hrs the French ship had lost her captain, Denieport, as well as her mizzenmast as a result of fighting with her British namesake and others. Her destruction came as a result of broadsides from the *Prince*, which set her foretop on fire. (National Maritime Museum)

STATISTICAL ANALYSIS

As is well known, Nelson succumbed to his wounds, but as he predicted, Trafalgar represented a decisive victory, thanks to the superior gunnery, discipline and seamanship of his crews. This is not to denigrate the courage and fortitude of the French and Spanish crews, who fought with greater spirit than expected and to whose bravery several contemporary British accounts of the action bear witness. Bravery was not enough, however, to offset the various disadvantages under which the Combined Fleet laboured, as analysis of the results of the battle reveals.

Evening at Trafalgar. The battle left a dreadful reckoning: 18 out of 33 ships of the Combined Fleet were captured or destroyed, together with perhaps 8,000 killed and wounded; the British lost no ships, but about 1,600 were killed and wounded. (National Maritime Museum)

FRENCH SHIP LOSSES AND CASUALTIES

The Combined Fleet lost 18 ships of the line at Trafalgar – nine French and nine Spanish, representing over half its strength. Seventeen of these vessels became prizes – though many of them were lost in the storm that wreaked havoc in the wake of the battle – and one, as just related, was destroyed by explosion. Statistics for casualties are less than perfect for the French and Spanish, since many men drowned in the subsequent storm, making it difficult to differentiate between casualties suffered in battle and those resulting from wrecked vessels. Estimated French losses may be summarized as follows:

A Spanish sailor. The majority of these men had no knowledge of deep-sea sailing, but rather of coastal waters only. Still, William Robinson admired the fighting qualities they exhibited at Trafalgar: '... it must be admitted that the Dons fought as well as the French in that battle; and if praise was due for seamanship and valour, they were well entitled to an equal share.' (Umhey Collection)

Killed: 1,425
Wounded: 1,410
Drowned: 2,296
Total: 5,131

Ordinarily, the disparity between killed and wounded would have been much greater – perhaps three times as many wounded as killed. The fact that the numbers were fairly equal may be accounted for by the almost complete loss of the crew of the *Achille*, with 480 officers and men killed. The *Bucentaure*, Villeneuve's flagship, lost 282 men, representing a third of her crew, while the *Redoutable* lost even more, though her sinking in the storm renders confirmation impossible. The disproportionate number of deaths to injuries may also be attributed to the fact that losses during the fighting mounted so quickly that surgeons were unable to treat the casualties fast enough to prevent large numbers of them succumbing to acute blood loss or shock. If battle casualties are tabulated, in distinction to those drowned in the subsequent storm, they total 20 per cent of the total complement of 14,000 officers and men aboard all French ships of the line. The total rises to a phenomenal 37 per cent if those drowned are included in the calculation. The average number of battle casualties aboard individual French ships was 157, though several vessels suffered more severely: besides the *Achille*, the *Redoutable* had perhaps 120 killed, 130 wounded and 275 subsequently drowned, a staggering total of 525 out of 643 officers and men. The unfortunate *Fougueux*, though she lost only 60 killed and 75 wounded in action, lost another 500 drowned, while the *Indomptable*, similarly, with 20 killed and 30 wounded, lost over 650 drowned.

SPANISH SHIP LOSSES AND CASUALTIES

The Spanish lost the same number of ships as the French, but suffered only half their losses – approximately 1,033 killed, 1,371 wounded and a smaller number (around 400) of drowned (most of the ships that foundered had their crews rescued by British ships escorting the prizes to Gibraltar). Space precludes details of every individual ship loss, but those suffering the heaviest casualties included the *Argonauta*, which had about 100 killed and 200 wounded; the *Monarca*, with approximately 100 killed and 150 wounded; the *San Agustín*, with about 180 killed and about 200 wounded; and the *Santísima Trinidad*, with about 200 killed, 100 wounded and an indeterminate number drowned in the storm. Best estimates for Spanish casualties total 2,404, approximately half those of their ally. Total combat losses for the Combined Fleet may therefore be calculated at 5,239. With Spanish crews amounting to approximately 12,000 men, the overall proportion of losses may be calculated at 20 per cent – slightly higher if the estimated number of drowned is correct – or approximately the same as for the French.

The rate of casualties between ships varied greatly: three ships suffered losses exceeding 300, while three others lost over 200 casualties. The *San Agustín* lost over half her complement, while the *Santísima Trinidad* lost nearly a third. On the other hand, the *San Justo* suffered no deaths and only seven wounded – the lightest casualties in the Combined Fleet. Average battle casualties amongst Spanish ships was 160 – very close to those of the French, with 157 (if the *Achille* is excepted). All told, including casualties suffered at Trafalgar and losses in the subsequent storm, the Combined Fleet lost about 8,000 men.

BRITISH CASUALTIES

The British lost no ships, though 11 were severely damaged, seven of which had to be towed to Gibraltar. Thus 40 per cent of Nelson's fleet was unable to perform further immediate service – tangible proof that the French and Spanish fought with determination and reasonable accuracy. Still, 14 British ships received only minor damage and remained in a position to fight and sail, as required, without a thorough refit in port, while two others received moderate damage. Those ships that had reached the enemy line first suffered the greatest damage, much of it inflicted during the long period of approach. Collingwood's column, though more numerous by three ships than Nelson's, sustained much greater damage – more than twice the number of losses – for the second-in-command had a tougher fight.

Nor had Nelson seriously to confront the van under Dumanoir who, it will be recalled, had failed – until a very late stage in the battle – to heed Villeneuve's signal to come about and assist the Franco-Spanish centre. Not only had Nelson been spared the necessity of having to fight him, the British commander-in-chief was gradually reinforced to the point that within an hour of the start of the battle, he actually outnumbered his opponents in the centre. Thus, while Nelson's column lost 161 killed and 377 wounded, for a total of 538 casualties, Collingwood's column had 297 killed and 831 wounded, a total of 1,128 casualties. Over half the losses (899) were shared between just six ships (*Victory*, *Téméraire*, *Royal Sovereign*, *Belleisle*, *Bellerophon* and *Colossus*), rendering the average loss per ship in the whole fleet at 62, with *Colossus* suffering the most (200) and *Prince* losing none at all – the only crew in the British fleet to emerge from the battle completely unscathed. Total British casualties were therefore 1,666, or about 10 per cent of the ships' overall complement of just above 17,000. This represents an exceptionally low figure for such a lengthy and hard-fought battle.

AFTERMATH

While Trafalgar marked the last fleet action of the Napoleonic Wars, there were other, less significant, though nonetheless important, naval engagements to follow: a year later, off Santo Domingo in the West Indies; a major raid on Aix and Basque Roads in the Bay of Biscay in 1809; and an encounter between British and French squadrons at Lissa, off the Adriatic coast, in 1811. The writing was, however, already on the wall for actions of this kind, for evidence of the decline of wooden navies was already apparent by the time of Trafalgar: only four years before, Robert Fulton had demonstrated to French naval authorities his crude, though reasonably effective method of destroying ships with a mine, and how steam could be successfully applied to shipping, naval as well as commercial. The last fleet action fought exclusively under sail took place at Navarino off the Greek coast in 1827, but by that time the debate of sail versus steam was already turning decisively in the latter's favour, thereby opening up new horizons for naval engineers, such as the potential of applying armour plating to vessels while still rendering them seaworthy. Only a decade after Navarino, in the first year of Victoria's reign, it was possible to travel almost the entire journey to India by virtue of steam power alone.

Traditionalists naturally continued to cling to sail power, not least on financial grounds: the Admiralty feared that the application of steam power to warships would render obsolete the entire Royal Navy. The authorities' hands were forced, however, when the French developed plans to build steam-powered warships, though such vessels rapidly revealed their own disadvantages: their great expense to build and maintain; the weight and bulk of coal that they had necessarily to carry, which greatly reduced the space

The battle of Navarino, 20 October 1827, when a combined British, French and Russian naval force annihilated the Turkish fleet during the War of Greek Independence. (Author's collection)

available for cargo and ammunition; and the greatest drawback of all – whereas sailing ships by definition drew on a limitless supply of power, steam ships conducting long voyages depended on strategically situated coaling stations for fuel. Moreover, while the rigging of a sailing vessel was naturally vulnerable to the strain imposed by wind and weather, damage was seldom extensive enough to make progress impossible. Mechanical failure aboard a ship bereft of sails, on the other hand, left it utterly immobilized, and thus for many years steam-driven ships, fitted with screws, were also sensibly rigged with sails. Still, the trend was

irreversible, and from the 1850s all capital ships of the Royal Navy employed steam power, though they continued to be constructed of wood, and it is noteworthy that the ships which conveyed troops to the Crimea, with their large decks, masts and square-rigging, still bore a strong resemblance to their forebears of half a century earlier.

The last wooden three-decker, HMS *Victoria*, was launched in 1859, but this was soon rendered obsolete by the introduction of steel-plated vessels, notably the French vessel *Gloire*, and the British reply, *Warrior*, hastily launched in 1860. The French then threatened to produce an ironclad – an innovation actually introduced simultaneously by the US Navy and the Confederacy – its superiority over wooden vessels being decisively demonstrated during the American Civil War (1861–65). The use of a turret aboard the USS *Monitor* meant that ships no longer had to depend on presenting their broadside to the enemy in order to fire, and with this feature – in conjunction with a fully-armoured hull – the forerunner of the modern battleship was born and the death knell of the wooden sailing ship rung.

Such radical changes in naval technology, only possible by industrialization on a grand scale, led to the rapid disappearance of masts, rigging, sails and wood in naval engineering, such that by the end of the century armour plating, revolving gun turrets deploying breech-loading 12-in. rifled guns and smoke-belching funnels became standard features amongst all modern navies. These steel monsters of the modern age, together with other innovations such as mines and submarines, the men of Trafalgar would not have believed possible.

Steam-powered warships of the Royal Navy making short shrift of Chinese junks during the First Opium War (1839–42). The advent of steam led to a revolution in naval warfare, for ships could operate with little concern for wind direction or speed and could thus reach any given theatre of operations in a fraction of the time required by vessels propelled entirely by sail. (Author's collection)

Ironclads in action: the epic contest between the USS *Monitor* and its Confederate counterpart the *Merrimac*, fought in 1862 off Hampton Roads, Virginia, during the American Civil War. The marriage of steam, exploding shells and armour plating would soon mark the end of wooden navies. (Author's collection)

BIBLIOGRAPHY

Adkin, Mark, *The Trafalgar Companion: The Complete Guide to History's Most Famous Sea Battle and the Life of Admiral Lord Nelson* (London, 2005)

Adkins, Roy, *Trafalgar: The Biography of a Battle* (London, 2004)

Ballantyne, Iain, and Jonathan Eastland, *HMS Victory* (London, 2005)

Best, Nicholas, *Trafalgar: The Untold Story of the Greatest Sea Battle in History* (London, 2005)

Blake, Nicholas, and Richard Lawrence, *The Illustrated Companion to Nelson's Navy* (London, 2003)

Clayton, Tim, and Phil Craig, *Trafalgar* (London, 2004)

Davies, David, *Fighting Ships: Ships of the Line, 1793–1815* (London, 1996)

Fraser, Edward, Marianne Cznik, and Michael Nash, *The Enemy at Trafalgar: Eyewitness Narratives, Dispatches and Letters from the French and Spanish Fleets* (London, 2004)

Fremont-Barnes, Gregory, *Nelson's Sailors* (Oxford, 2005)

Fremont-Barnes, Gregory, *Trafalgar 1805: Nelson's Crowning Victory* (Oxford, 2005)

Fremont-Barnes, Gregory, *The Royal Navy, 1793–1815* (Oxford, 2007)

Gardiner, Robert, ed., *The Campaign of Trafalgar, 1803–1805* (London, 1997)

Gardiner, Robert, ed., *The Line of Battle: The Sailing Warship, 1650–1840* (Annapolis, MD, 1992)

Gardiner, Robert, *Warships of the Napoleonic Era* (London, 2003)

Goodwin, Peter, *Men O'War: The Illustrated Story of Life in Nelson's Navy* (London, 2004)

Goodwin, Peter, *Nelson's Victory: 101 Questions and Answers about HMS Victory, Nelson's Flagship at Trafalgar 1805* (London, 2004)

Goodwin, Peter, *The Ships of Trafalgar: The British, French and Spanish Fleets, 21 October 1805* (London, 2004)

Harbron, John, *Trafalgar and the Spanish Navy: The Spanish Experience of Sea Power* (London, 2004)

Harland, John, *Seamanship in the Age of Sail* (London, 1984)

Heathcote, T. A., *Nelson's Trafalgar Captains and their Battles* (London, 2005)

Howard, Frank, *Sailing Ships of War, 1400–1860* (London, 1979)

Ireland, Bernard, *Naval Warfare in the Age of Sail: War at Sea, 1756–1815* (New York, 2000)

Lambert, Andrew, *War at Sea in the Age of Sail* (London, 2000)

Lavery, Brian, *The Arming and Fitting of English Ships of War, 1600–1815* (London, 1999)

Lavery, Brian, *The Line of Battle: The Sailing Warship, 1650–1840*, 2 vols (London, 1992)

Lavery, Brian, *Nelson's Fleet at Trafalgar* (Annapolis, MD, 2004)

Lavery, Brian, *Nelson's Navy: The Ships, Men and Organisation, 1793–1815* (London, 1989)

Lavery, Brian, *Jack Aubrey Commands: An Historical Companion to the Naval World of Patrick O'Brian* (London, 2003)

Lavery, Brian, *The Ship of the Line. Vol. 1: The Development of the Battlefleet, 1650–1850* (London, 1984)

Lavery, Brian, *The Ship of the Line: Vol. 2: Design, Construction, and Fittings*, 2 vols (London, 1997)

LeFevre, Peter, *Nelson's Fleet at Trafalgar* (Annapolis, MD, 2004)

Lewis, Jon, ed., *The Mammoth Book of How it Happened: Trafalgar* (London, 2005)

Maynard, C., ed., *A Nelson Companion: A Guide to the Royal Navy of Jack Aubrey* (London, 2004)

McGowan, Alan, HMS *Victory: Her Construction, Career and Restoration* (London, 1999)

McKay, John, *100 Gun Ship "Victory"* (London, 2000)

Nicolson, Adam, *Men of Honour: Trafalgar and the Making of the English Hero* (London, 2005)

Pocock, Tom. *Trafalgar: An Eyewitness History* (London: Penguin, 2005)

Pope, Dudley, *England Expects: Nelson and the Trafalgar Campaign* (London, 1999)

Pope, Dudley, *Life in Nelson's Navy* (London, 1997)

Pope, Stephen, *Hornblower's Navy: Life at Sea in the Age of Nelson* (London, 1998)

Robson, Martin, *Battle of Trafalgar* (London, 2005)

Rodger, N. A. M., *Command of the Ocean: A Naval History of Britain, 1649–1815* (London, 2006)

Schom, Alan, *Trafalgar: Countdown to Battle, 1803–1805* (London, 1992)

Smith, Digby, *Navies of the Napoleonic Era* (London, 2004)

Tunstall, Brian, *Naval Warfare in the Age of Sail: The Evolution of Fighting Tactics, 1650–1815*. Edited by Nicholas Tracy (Annapolis, MD, 1990)

Warner, Oliver, *Trafalgar* (London, 1966)

Warwick, Peter, *Voices from Trafalgar* (London, 2005)

Winfield, Rif, *British Warships in the Age of Sail, 1792–1815: Design, Construction, Career and Fates* (London, 2005)

INDEX

References to illustrations are shown in **bold**.